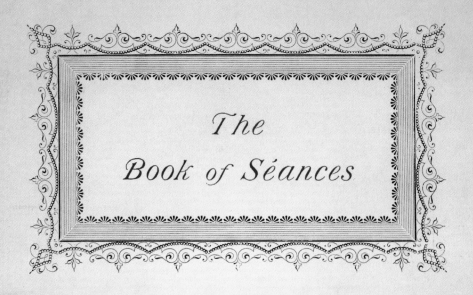

The Book of Séances

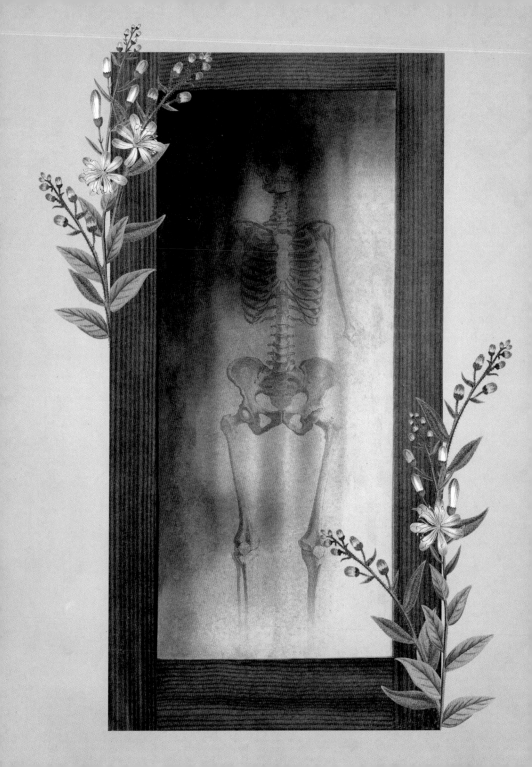

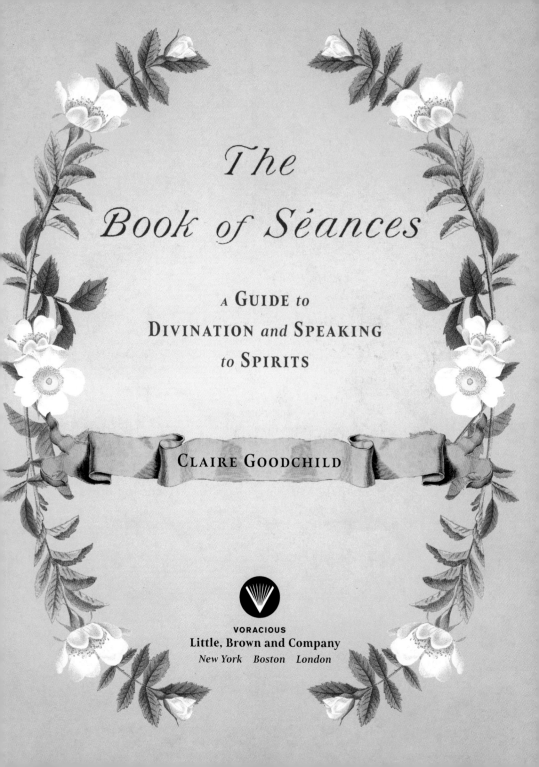

The Book of Séances

A GUIDE to DIVINATION and SPEAKING to SPIRITS

CLAIRE GOODCHILD

VORACIOUS
Little, Brown and Company
New York   Boston   London

Voracious / Little, Brown and Company
Hachette Book Group
1290 Avenue of the Americas, New York, NY 10104
littlebrown.com

FIRST EDITION: October 2022

Voracious is an imprint of Little, Brown and Company, a division of Hachette Book Group,
Inc. The Voracious name and logo are trademarks of Hachette Book Group, Inc.

The publisher is not responsible for websites
(or their content) that are not owned by the publisher.

The Hachette Speakers Bureau provides a wide range of authors for speaking events.
To find out more, go to hachettespeakersbureau.com or call (866) 376-6591.

Designed by Leah Carlson-Stanisic

ISBN 9780316353342
LCCN 2022936431

10 9 8 7 6 5 4 3 2 1

tc

Printed in Canada

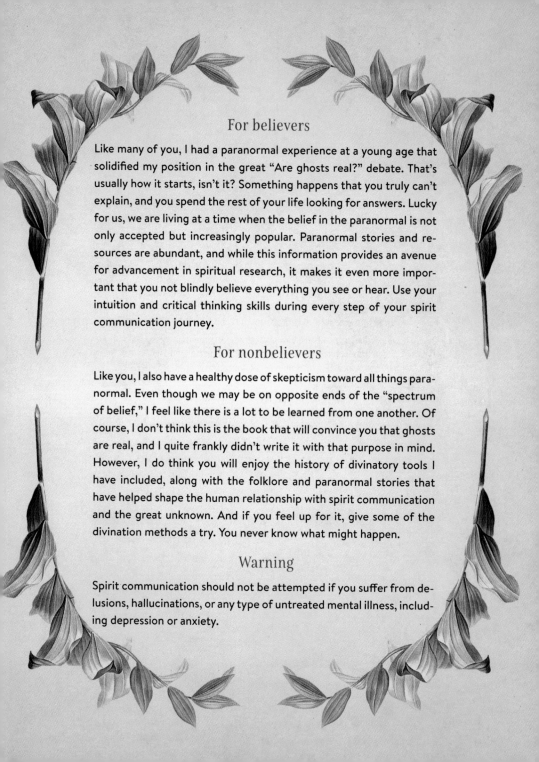

For believers

Like many of you, I had a paranormal experience at a young age that solidified my position in the great "Are ghosts real?" debate. That's usually how it starts, isn't it? Something happens that you truly can't explain, and you spend the rest of your life looking for answers. Lucky for us, we are living at a time when the belief in the paranormal is not only accepted but increasingly popular. Paranormal stories and resources are abundant, and while this information provides an avenue for advancement in spiritual research, it makes it even more important that you not blindly believe everything you see or hear. Use your intuition and critical thinking skills during every step of your spirit communication journey.

For nonbelievers

Like you, I also have a healthy dose of skepticism toward all things paranormal. Even though we may be on opposite ends of the "spectrum of belief," I feel like there is a lot to be learned from one another. Of course, I don't think this is the book that will convince you that ghosts are real, and I quite frankly didn't write it with that purpose in mind. However, I do think you will enjoy the history of divinatory tools I have included, along with the folklore and paranormal stories that have helped shape the human relationship with spirit communication and the great unknown. And if you feel up for it, give some of the divination methods a try. You never know what might happen.

Warning

Spirit communication should not be attempted if you suffer from delusions, hallucinations, or any type of untreated mental illness, including depression or anxiety.

Introduction . . . ix

PART ONE

1 **What Is Death?** ... 3
Who is Claire? About this book.

2 **What Is Divination?** ... 17
The three types of divination
covered in this book: casting, scrying, and
channeling.

3 **What Are Séances and**
Spiritualism? ... 29
What is a séance? What is spiritualism?
What happened with the Fox sisters?

4 **The Other Side** ... 43
What is a spirit? What is a ghost?
What types of entities exist? Are there
different realms? Who can communicate
with the dead? What are the three clairs?
What is a medium?

5 **How to Perform**
a Séance ... 65
How do you perform a séance? Are
séances dangerous? How can readers
protect themselves? Should they keep
records? What is a sacred space? Should
séances be performed in a group or alone?

PART TWO

6 **Cartomancy** ... 85
What is cartomancy?
An instructional.

7 **Automatic Writing** ... 135
What is automatic writing?
An instructional.

8 **Bibliomancy** ... 149
What is bibliomancy?
An instructional.

9 **Spirit Board** ... 167
What is a spirit board?
An instructional.

10 **Tasseography** ... 185
What is tasseography?
An instructional.

Contents

11 Rhabdomancy ... 213
What is rhabdomancy?
An instructional.

12 A Scientific Séance ... 227
Modern tools, the history of
EVP, and spirit photography.
An instructional.

13 More Types of Casting
Divination ... 239
Charm casting and domino reading.
An instructional.

14 More Types of Scrying
Divination ... 261
Mirror scrying and candle scrying.
An instructional.

15 Caring for Your Tools ...
279
How do you take care of your divinatory
objects?
An instructional.

Acknowledgments ... 285

Glossary ... 287

INTRODUCTION

There are many challenges to researching and writing a guide about how to communicate with spirits through different methods of divination.

For one, psychics and mediums can feel like their gifts are being mocked, making them less likely to share their secrets—something that has happened repeatedly throughout history. Likewise, paranormal investigators can be cagey, unwilling to share their methodologies except with those who adhere exactly to the strict parameters of their prescribed scientific procedures.

The truth is that communion with the spirits lies at the crossroads of spirituality and science.

I believe that we are at this moment collectively embarking on a new journey in terms of spirit communication and paranormal investigating— one with more room for a range of spirit communication techniques and an array of different ideas about ghosts. Some techniques will be scientific, and some will be spiritual. This journey will be more about building connections with our loved ones than about proving their otherworldly existence to the masses. I feel that this balanced approach allows everyone to participate and decide what is real for themselves.

A large part of working with the other side effectively is about understanding your own belief systems. It is about taking stock of what approaches do and don't seem credible to you.

Chances are this is not your first divination book, and maybe it's not even your first spirit communication book.

I don't claim to know everything. I am only sharing what I have learned from years of research, personal experiences, and experimentation. I am a practicing witch, and many of my beliefs about death and spirits are rooted in folk magic practices.

There may be things in this book that contradict what you have previously learned. There may be things in this book that don't speak to you, and there may be things in this book that you really connect with. My aim has been to provide you with one or more pieces of the puzzle to show you new ways to build your relationships with people on the other side.

You don't need to be a full-time paranormal investigator, or a medium, or even a witch in order to communicate with spirits.

You just need to learn how to use divinatory tools and interpret the messages you receive.

As long as you have patience, dedication, and compassion, you can hold your very own séances.

This book will teach you how.

—Claire

PART ONE

1

What Is Death?

This is a question we carry around with us every single day. Because we are aware of our own mortality, death influences the choices we make, whether we are actively thinking about it or not.

As human beings, we automatically do what we can to hold off death as long as possible. We seek out food, water, and shelter. We live together in communities and protect one another. And sometimes we even inflict death on others in the hope that we can avoid our own.

To be dead means that we are not alive, and staying alive is our most basic instinct.

The irony is that when these survival needs are met, we are freed up to ponder death. Secure in our safety, we begin to focus our attention on understanding *why* death happens, and where we go when it does.

Death gets the full biological and spiritual examination.

WHAT DO WE KNOW ABOUT DEATH?

It is universal: Everything that is living dies. For some creatures, like mayflies, life and death happen in a span of twenty-four hours, while other creatures, like Greenland sharks, can live for hundreds of years.

It is irreversible: Everything that dies stays dead (except in cases of medical revival). As far as we know, you can't be dead for thirty years, and then come back to life in your body and resume living the way you did before.

It is nonfunctional: When you die, all living functions stop. Your organs no longer work and your consciousness ends.

It's this last point (nonfunctionality) that is challenged by a belief in an afterlife. Regardless of our religious or spiritual associations, everyone who believes that there is something else beyond what we see must also believe that there is some type of functionality after death.

For spiritualists—a group of people you will learn a lot about in this book—the consciousness and the soul of a person are one and the same. It's this consciousness that can interact with the living through a variety of spirit communication techniques that were established over the last hundred years and which I will be teaching you in this book.

DEATH AS ITS OWN STATE OF BEING

The boundaries which divide life from death are at best shadowy and vague. Who shall say where the one ends, and where the other begins?

Edgar Allan Poe said it best in this excerpt from his story "The Premature Burial." These two lines serve as a reminder that death is not only an ending to one state of being but also its *own* state of being. A state that we exist in longer than any other.

I like to explain the idea of being in multiple life-and-death states in the following way because it is easy to picture.

Let's say that you have a beautiful pothos plant and you want to propagate it in order to create more. So you cut a stem off the plant and place it in water, where soon it begins to grow roots.

Before you know it, this new piece of the plant is living happily in a pot in a sunny corner of your home.

But suddenly the original part of the plant, the one that grew from seed and not through propagation, dies. Does that mean both plants are now dead?

The plant still exists, doesn't it?

It exists in its dead state—all dry and brown and withered—but it also exists in a living state in the form of the second plant.

Its life force has transformed from one state into multiple states. The plant is simultaneously gone and not gone.

THE HEART OF THE MATTER

There is a phenomenon that humans deal with on a regular basis that is quite similar to the propagation example, and that is memory transfer via organ transplant.

For as long as we have been transplanting organs, recipients have been reporting strange and unusual side effects.

There is a medical hypothesis that says, "The acquisition of donor personality characteristics by recipients following heart transplantation is hypothesized to occur via the transfer of cellular memory" (Mitchell B. Liester, "Personality Changes Following Heart Transplantation: The Role of Cellular Memory," *Medical Hypotheses*, Feb. 2020).

Basically, this means that in some cases when someone receives a heart transplant, they also inherit parts of the donor's personality. They report their personal taste preferences changing across a wide range of areas, such as favorite foods and music.

It is thought that memory is stored not only in the brain but inside *all* our cells.

Claire Sylvia, one of the first people to receive a heart and lung transplant, documented in her memoir that after she inherited the organs of an eighteen-year-old boy, she began craving foods she never wanted before, such as beer and cheeseburgers.

Claire's family and friends also remarked that even her walk had changed.

This transfer of memory raises questions about the medical definition of death. If we are our consciousness, and part of that consciousness can be put into another person…are we dead when we die?

DEFINITIONS OF DEATH

Legally dead

Depending on where you live in the world, the legal definition of death may differ, but in most places it is when the brain no longer functions independently. This is because the brain controls every other biological function.

Because the legal definition of brain death varies, the term often raises a question about whether people in comas or vegetative states are legally dead. The answer is: maybe.

Most physicians agree that in order to be brain-dead, there must be permanent damage to the area of the brain stem leading to a complete cessation of breathing ability.

However, some coma patients suffer damage to the area of the brain stem that controls breathing and require medical assistance to breathe, only to heal, regain function, and continue living.

While people who are in a brain-dead state are dead, their body's mechanisms can function with the intervention of medical equipment. But if you remove this equipment, the body ceases all function once again and decomposes.

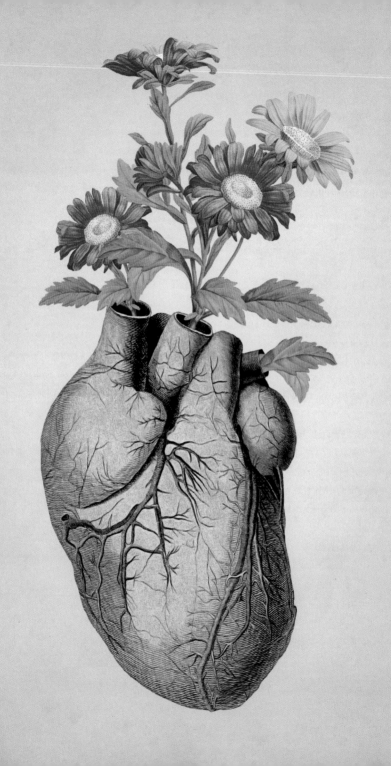

Clinically dead

Clinically dead is when a person's heart stops beating but their brain has enough blood and oxygen to keep working for a short period of time. A person can sometimes be brought back to life with medical intervention such as CPR. However, if the heart fails to restart, the brain will soon be starved of blood and oxygen and will stop working.

DEATH CUSTOMS

All cultures have their own ways of handling death. Some of these practices have been the same for hundreds, even thousands, of years, while others have evolved and changed over time.

There is value in learning about these different processes, even if they sometimes make us feel uncomfortable. This discomfort is felt most often by Westerners, as we have made dying a very impersonal thing. Death has been hidden away, labeled as taboo, despite the fact that it is such a normal part of living.

Ancient Egypt

It's impossible to think of death customs and not think of the Ancient Egyptians. There is a reason people have remained fascinated with the culture for so long; between the linen-wrapped mummies and the colossal pyramids, it's hard not to be.

The afterlife in Ancient Egypt is a place known as the Field of Reeds (or Field of Offerings). Here there is no pain, no suffering—only joy.

In order to get to the Field of Reeds, your body and spirit must undergo a plethora of funeral rites.

Egyptians believed that the *ba* (soul) could not survive without the *ka* (body), and therefore great effort was made to preserve a person after they died.

The mummification process began with a ritual washing of the body. This would be done with water from the Nile River, which was considered sacred.

Next, any organs that could speed up the decomposition process were removed and placed in canopic jars. These would be buried with the person, so they had access to them in the afterlife.

The heart always remained inside the body, as it was considered to be where the soul lived.

After these tasks were performed, the body would be posed and preserved with natron or bitumen. Part of the posing involved opening the mouth to ensure that the person would have the ability to speak when they arrived in the Field of Reeds.

Next, the body would be wrapped in linen bandages, which would then be elaborately decorated with various charms.

And finally, the body would be placed in a sarcophagus and buried.

The process took anywhere from sixty to eighty days, and while all this work was being done, the family would mourn.

The Ancient Egyptians made a great show of mourning. Public displays were encouraged, and sometimes female mourners were even hired to aid in this part of the process. They would tear their clothes, wail, and even rub dirt on their faces and breasts.

After the body was buried, the family of the deceased would frequently visit the tombs and burial places of their loved ones and throw elaborate parties. They would also sometimes create altars inside their homes where they would communicate with the person.

Tibetan sky burials

In Tibet, a sky burial is a traditional Buddhist custom where, upon death, the body is taken into the mountains and fed to vultures.

When a person dies, their body is kept in the home for three to five days, and during this time, monks will chant prayers and read scripture in order to prevent the soul from being caught in purgatory.

When the appropriate amount of time has passed, the family of the deceased will collectively decide on the most auspicious day for the burial, known as the lucky day.

The body is then disrobed and put in the fetal position before being placed in a special body bag.

From there, it is carried up the mountain by the body carrier (also known as the body breaker). The body carrier is typically a monk from a nearby monastery. The family of the deceased do not attend the sky burial, but congregate nearby and pray.

The body carrier then dismembers the body, and vultures are lured toward it with a special incense.

Receiving a sky burial is a huge honor. If the vultures, which are holy birds, eat all the flesh, then the deceased has no sins and is able to proceed to heaven.

Luckily, if part of the body does remain, the monks have a ritual they perform in order to help the soul cross over.

When only bones remain, the body carrier breaks them with a mallet and mixes them with a special barley flour called tsampa, and then that too is fed to the vultures.

The most interesting part of this custom is that everything is done with joy and laughter. It is believed that this helps the soul transition to the afterlife. Even while in mourning, the family understands the importance of giving the spirit of their loved one the best funeral experience possible.

Turning of the bones in Madagascar

The Malagasy people of the island Madagascar, just off the coast of Africa east of Mozambique, have an unusual and incredible ritual they perform for the dead that spans years.

It is called Famadihana, which means "the turning of the bones."

The Malagasy believe that the soul does not move on to the afterlife as long as the body still remains here on Earth.

Held every few years, Famadihana is performed not only to speed up the decomposition process but also to honor the dead. It gives new family members (such as babies and in-laws) a chance to meet and interact with their ancestors.

During the celebration, the dead are wrapped in new cloth, danced with, and given gifts, such as lipstick or cologne, before being returned to the tomb.

In recent years, Famadihana has faced a lot of criticism from government officials due to the possibility that the celebration could aid in the spread of pneumonic plague, the deadliest form of the illness there is.

It will be interesting to see if Famadihana evolves to help remedy this growing concern, or if it will remain as it always has been.

DEATH AS MY COMPANION (ABOUT ME)

As a child, my weekends were spent with my two sisters exploring the woods surrounding my grandparents' home just north of Toronto. Summer gave us toads to catch and never-ending games of tag. Spring was for foraging newly sprung buds for potions we made for the fairies. Winter was about bold expeditions into the vast expansion of snow, and autumn...well, autumn brought with it all it really knows: death.

The afternoon in November in which my whole world changed was unseasonably warm, but my sisters and I weren't tramping around the fallen leaves like usual. No, we were playing with my new clown doll in the sitting room. I had just received it as a gift from a friend, and felt an immediate connection to it. Everything from his little patterned outfit to his porcelain face was perfect. I had always liked clowns, and he was no different.

My younger sister was playing with me, while my older sister sat by the window reading a book. She was getting to the age where dolls were not very interesting, and playing with your younger sisters was even less so.

I don't know what compelled us to play the game we did, and in the moment it seemed harmless. How were we supposed to know what was about to happen?

Children's imaginations are complex things. They piece together bits of information from television, parents, and friends. Playing pretend is a form of problem-solving, figuring out how the world works. My sisters and I had absolutely no experience with ambulances or emergency services, but that afternoon we decided to play paramedics.

Clown doll was in full cardiac arrest and needed to get to the hospital ASAP.

He wasn't going to make it—I knew this. It was pre-planted in my nine-year-old mind. I was the head paramedic, and my younger assistant was not going to be the one to save him.

Our chest compressions were interrupted by my grandmother coming into the room to tell us that lunch would be ready shortly. We were to wash our hands and put away our toys while she called for my grandfather, who was working away in the garage.

When he hadn't come up a few minutes later, my grandmother walked down the small hill to get him. Thinking he just had the radio on too loud, she was shocked to find him slumped on the ground, blocking the door.

Things get a little blurry here. There is a chunk of time missing between the real paramedics arriving and us three girls kneeling on the couch, all in a row, watching them try to revive our grandfather from the window, knowing that he was already gone.

I don't know what happened to that clown doll. By the time the ambulance left, he was gone from the spot where I had left him, and he has never been found. Needless to say, my fondness for clowns quickly morphed into distaste.

It may surprise you to learn that that day wasn't the last time I saw my grandfather.

Over the years, I would wake up in the middle of the night to see him hunched over a desk, writing, or toiling away in the garden at the back of the property, only to vanish as soon as I got near.

I don't see him that often now. Whether that is a symptom of my age or just the amount of time he's been gone, I do not know. I may catch a glimpse of him in the mirror or a shadow passing by the window, and it's oddly comforting to know he is still there in some form, even if it is just a memory imprint on the environment.

After this experience, death became my constant companion. I would see and hear things that my parents didn't seem to notice. Nothing scary like you see in movies. It was little things like muffled conversations or the sound of a door closing when it was open right in front of you.

I should mention here that I don't think my experiences are unique. I believe all people are witnesses to ghost activity, but some are just paying more attention to it.

Most people I have spoken to who also believe in ghosts recall a major incident similar to what happened to me with the clown doll. An incident that *forced* them to pay closer attention to these things.

By the time I was eleven, I had a handle on ignoring these "things" when I needed to. I didn't talk about them in order to avoid drawing any more attention to myself. My school days were plagued with bullying and often ended with me in tears. I knew that talking about ghosts would place an even larger target on my back.

It was around this time that my mother's friend suggested that I try Wicca. I was immediately enthralled. Here was this set of beliefs that told me I had personal power. Power that could be merged with energies surrounding us. Energy that lived in the trees and rocks, the wind and sea.

This was in 1999, and the internet as we know it was just in its infancy, but that didn't stop me from devouring every online resource I could find over the next few years. I didn't understand all the material I was reading, but I understood how empowered it made me feel.

By age twenty or twenty-one, I began to look outside Wicca and into other forms of witchcraft, which opened up even more experiences. It was during this time that I began practicing different forms of divination, as well as working with different ideas surrounding death and the afterlife.

Cartomancy was something that I immediately took to, but there was one problem: the decks I was seeing didn't speak to my personal tastes.

During this time, I had been working for different photographers doing photo retouching, and one of them taught me photo restoration. I felt at home manipulating the antique photos back to their former glory, and began experimenting with making collages outside of work using images from old medical texts featuring skeletons. This is how my debut tarot deck, the Antique Anatomy Tarot, was born.

Since then, my focus has remained on spirit communication, ancestor work, and folk magic, all of which I have blended into my subsequent oracle decks, art, and writing.

I believe the dead have valuable things to teach us; we just don't always know how to listen for an answer.

2

What Is Divination?

For most people, hearing the word "divination" conjures up images of carnival fortune-tellers, or a group of kids sitting around a Ouija board scaring themselves.

Everyone has different levels of experience when it comes to divination, but most of us do it in one way or another. For some, reading a horoscope in the morning is the extent of their practice, while others don't make any decision without consulting their tarot cards.

WHAT IS DIVINATION?

Divination is the art of interpreting signs and symbols in order to gain knowledge about the unknown. It is a broad definition that encompasses many different practices. Some are highly complex systems, such as astrology, while others are more simple and intuitive, such as interpreting weather patterns.

Divination began as a way for our earliest ancestors to understand how the world works. In order to not only survive but also thrive as a society, they needed to make sense of why certain things seemed to happen. By anticipating challenges and obstacles, people were able to plan ahead and ensure that they had appropriate resources available. This process was equivalent to a spiritual earthquake kit. Divination was about recognizing patterns and cycles, and combining those with supernatural or intuitive knowledge, then making predictions for the future.

Thus, divination became a part of daily life. There were simple rituals that were utilized by everyone, as well as complicated daylong affairs that were performed by priests and priestesses.

Divination can be grouped into various categories, with animal divination positioned as one of the most important from a historical standpoint.

Animal signs

The relationship between humans and animals is a sacred one. We rely on them not only for food and farming but also to teach us about how the world works.

One method used by both the Greeks and the Romans was haruspicy. This process involved sacrificing an animal, usually a sheep or a fowl, and then analyzing their entrails in order to make predictions. There was a belief that the liver held special significance. If it appeared healthy, a period of positivity and abundance was on the horizon, but if it was discolored or oddly shaped, doom was sure to follow.

This may seem gruesome to us today, but animals have always played a big part in divination. However, not all of their involvement was of a sacrificial nature.

For the Dogon tribe of West Africa, the jackal is a figure seen repeatedly in mythology and divinatory practices. Dogon elders will set up rectangles made of stones, lure the jackals into the pens with peanuts, and then interpret the patterns left by their paw prints inside the stone boundaries during the night.

If you live in a colder climate, you are well aware of the migratory patterns of birds. The time they leave and the time they return can give us clues to the upcoming season, but weather isn't the only thing birds are used to predict.

The Ancient Greeks relied on the behavior of birds to forecast a wide range of events, the most important being war. Birds of prey were of special significance,

and the direction they flew could determine how successful a battle would be. Larger birds, such as eagles and vultures, were thought to contain specific messages from the gods.

And of course no animal divination would be complete without the art of reading bones, a practice that is found across the world. This practice required symbols and signs to be carved into small animal bones and then interpreted.

While I don't think you should go and sacrifice an animal before practicing divination, I do suggest incorporating animal energy into your sessions in the form of a good luck charm, such as a figurine or image.

Planetary partners

Earth and her ever-changing seasons, and the messages delivered from the stars and planets, were also used for divinatory purposes.

The most famous of these celestial forms of divination is astrology. Ancient forms of astrology appear in Egypt, Mesoamerica, Greece, China, and elsewhere.

However, there are other forms of divination that utilize the natural world.

One of these is geomancy, which is a Greek word meaning "divination by earth."

Geomancy is found in many regions, and can involve physical objects such as gemstones, rocks, and soil, or it can be more energetic in nature, much like feng shui.

The most well-known type of geomancy is an ancient Arab system that relies on sophisticated mathematical calculations traced in the sand, which are then interpreted. It is thought that this system is the precursor of many other forms of geomancy found in Europe and Africa.

WHY USE DIVINATION?

People use divination to predict the future, to reveal something otherwise unknown, and to communicate with spirits. People use divination to get advice, make predictions, and gain insight about the past, present, or future.

To predict the future

Divination can be used to predict the outcome of a situation if all the current forces and influences surrounding the scenario stay on their current course.

One important thing to remember is that the future is not fixed, and different twists and turns can change it at any time. Divination is about preparing yourself for a possibility. The outcome should not be the only factor you look at when making a decision. Your mood, your short-term and long-term goals, as well as any outside influences—like other people—should be considered alongside the outcome prediction.

What feels important one day may not the next. This is why divination is a continuous practice: as you evolve, your practice evolves with you.

To reveal the unknown

When divination is used to reveal something, it is about looking at a situation from a new perspective in order to make a sound and well-rounded decision. We all have our internal biases, and these influence every decision we make. Divination is about finding balance between our logical side and our intuitive side.

To communicate with spirits

Divination for spirit communication is a little bit different. Predictions and revealing the unknown come into play, but so do other people's consciousnesses. Spirit communication can be used to gather advice, but also as a bonding exercise between yourself and your loved ones, living and deceased.

Divination with the purpose of communicating with the spirit of a deceased person is known as necromancy.

The term "necromancy" makes many people nervous, and that is quite understandable, as there have been deliberate attempts to present necromancy in a negative light.

In medieval Europe, there was a big push by the church to label all occult practices—especially necromancy—as inherently evil. Despite this, it still found legions of practitioners, many of whom were members of the clergy themselves.

However, like all other forms of divination, spirit communication is not rooted in negativity. The energy is neutral, and it is the intent of the reader that sets its course.

> NOTE: Some forms of necromancy can involve a person reanimating a corpse or controlling a spirit in order to perform tasks; this is not what we are learning in this book.

DIVINATION TERMINOLOGY

While techniques may vary, all forms of divination generally involve asking a question and receiving an answer.

Reading: A reading is the act of using divination to gain insight. For example, when you ask a deck of tarot cards a question and then draw a card at random for the answer, that is a reading.

For our purposes, a séance, or session, is the same as a reading but with the added element of communicating with spirits. It is about having a conversation rather than just receiving advice about a situation.

Reader: The reader is the person who performs the reading.

Querent: The querent is the person asking the question or the one seeking answers. The querent and the reader are often the same person.

Tip: If you are reading for another person, be sure to say things as you see them, even if it seems strange or unusual. Divination is extremely personal, and something that makes no sense to you can mean everything to someone else.

HOW TO USE THIS BOOK

The divination methods in this book have been chosen for a variety of reasons.

Practicality and accessibility

The first and most important reason is that these methods work very well for spirit communication. Some were created specifically for this purpose, while others were adapted for this work during the height of the spiritualism movement in the nineteenth century.

Not only can they be used in a paranormal sense; they can also be used for regular or "traditional" readings, such as when asking advice or making predictions. At the beginning of any session, decide what type of reading you will be doing. Some people ask for spirits to communicate only when invited, while other people are open to spirits participating in all readings.

The second reason is that the methods of divination in this book are accessible to a broad range of people. There is something here that will suit everyone's personal preferences, skill level, and budget. Even if you cannot purchase a deck of cards or a pair of divining rods, chances are you have access to a book for bibliomancy or a teacup for tasseography.

DIVINATION CATEGORIES

For the purposes of this book, the divination categories we are using are casting, scrying, and channeling. Every method you encounter in the second half of this book can be loosely placed into one or more of these categories.

Casting

Casting divination is the act of sorting or shuffling items and either choosing or distributing them at random in order to receive an answer. Casting is also known as sortilege.

Example: Sorting and choosing domino tiles at random and then using numerology to interpret the message is a form of casting.

Scrying

To scry means to see into the future. Scrying is seeing something revealed on the surface of another thing. The surface is usually, but not always, reflective.

Example: Though not reflective, reading tea leaves is a form of scrying as you are seeing images on the surface of a cup.

Channeling

Channeling is the act of receiving messages from the spirit world.

Example: When performing any type of spirit communication, you are effectively participating in a form of channeling.

Spirit communication is always a form of channeling, whether the energy is being channeled by your physical body or by the tools you're using.

WORKING THROUGH THIS BOOK

Although the instructions in the book are geared toward spirit communication, all these methods of divination are suitable for any type of reading.

I recommend working through each chapter of this book in order. Presenting cartomancy as the first method was a deliberate choice. Tarot reading is wildly popular, so the tools are easier to find than, say, sternomancy—which is interpreting the color and shape of the sternum of a corpse. The tarot is also very well suited for spirit communication.

Be sure to spend a minimum of three months on each divining method before deciding it isn't for you.

If you are more experienced with divination or spirit work, you may find it helpful to modify any of the instructions to better suit your needs. You may also find that combining more than one type of divination works well.

Some suggested pairings:

Tasseography & Charm Casting—
see if any symbols repeat.

Cartomancy & Domino Casting—
see if any numbers repeat.

Automatic Writing & Bibliomancy—
see if any words or phrases repeat.

Some of these divination methods will challenge your preexisting beliefs and ask you to explore situations from a new perspective. Take time to observe and reflect on any feelings that arise during this process.

Working with spirits through divination can be extremely rewarding, but it does require dedication and a reasonable amount of effort.

Divination for spirit communication is about building a mutual relationship between you and a spirit. Spirits are not just personal servants who do or say what you want, when you want. Have reasonable expectations for not only yourself but the souls you are communicating with.

Remember: While I do encourage you to challenge yourself, it should not be at the expense of your safety or emotional well-being. If you don't feel comfortable with a particular form of divination in this book, you do not need to attempt it.

Stay safe and have fun!

3

What Are Séances and Spiritualism?

In the West, we do everything possible to keep death hidden away. We sanitize it with euphemisms like "the big sleep" or "with the Lord." But it wasn't always this way. In the 1800s and early 1900s, people invited the dead back into their homes…in the form of séances.

WHAT ARE SÉANCES?

"Séance" comes from the French word for "session."

A séance is an attempt by an individual or a group of people to contact and communicate with the spirits of the dead. It could be a big religious affair or a small informal session consisting of one to three people.

Rituals like this exist around the world, but the ones I am referencing are those that specifically took place in the United States, Canada, and Western Europe beginning in the 1800s and 1900s.

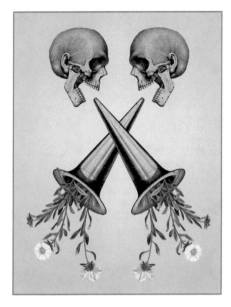

Traditionally, a séance is a reading involving a group of participants led by a medium, who provides a direct energetic link to the other side. (For more on mediums, see page 57.)

The people who most often engaged in séances were known as the spiritualists (more on them in a moment).

TABLE TURNING

When asked to picture a séance, most people immediately think of a table-turning session. This is where a group of people sit around a table holding hands in a room illuminated by only candles. The medium or leader of the séance asks for a spirit to make its presence known by knocking, moving, or even lifting the table.

Table turning likely evolved from a form of informal séance where a small group would gather around a table in someone's home to hear messages channeled by a medium. As séances grew in popularity, mediums had to create more and more elaborate experiences to attract customers.

This led to the use of different devices and techniques, such as spirit trumpets. A spirit trumpet is a freestanding skinny metal cone—think of an ice cream cone—that could be used by a medium to amplify the soft whispers of a spirit. It's reported that these trumpets would float around the room looking for someone to speak into them...controlled by the spirit, of course.

LARGE-GROUP AND STAGE SÉANCES

"Who's the J name?" the medium asks the
audience. A woman, tears in her eyes, raises her
hand. "That must be my husband, James!"

We have all seen these sorts of séances on TV, or perhaps we have even attended one. The stage séance is something that developed in the nineteenth century and has actually never left us. Stage séances are performed by mediums for a large audience, and it is thought that during the session, different spirits will come forward with messages consisting of symbols, and they must be deciphered by the group.

A word of warning: Much of honest spirit communication involves deciphering symbols, and this is what we will cover in the second half of this book. However, you must be very careful about which mediums you believe in. Many swindlers use a technique known as cold reading, in which they send out a bunch of vague messages and see which one resonates based on the body language of their audience. These people are not doing this to create connection; they are doing it to make money, and should be avoided. If you would like to work with a medium, be sure to do lots of research in order to find someone reputable.

Mesmerism and showmanship were a big part of the stage séance. The Davenport brothers, who frequently held stage séances, made use of a specially crafted piece of furniture called a spirit cabinet.

Their spirit cabinet was a large wooden cabinet that the brothers would sit inside, one at each end, facing each other. An audience member would be picked to securely tie them in place and the doors would be closed. Next the doors would be opened and the brothers would appear to have been freed from their ropes by aid of spirits. Then the doors would be closed again, and reopened to show them magically tied back up.

Not everyone liked the Davenport brothers. Many felt that they made a mockery of real mediumship and séances. There were numerous occasions when they were assaulted after their show, and one time, their spirit cabinet was broken into bits.

Not only did the spectators give them a hard time; the law did as well. They were fined and jailed more than once.

However, this didn't dissuade other mediums from making their own spirit cabinets and specialized props in order to create grand illusions. In fact, many of today's magicians and illusionists have spiritualism to thank for their contribution to the art of stage magic.

SMALL-GROUP AND SOLO SÉANCES

As spiritualism grew in popularity, people began experimenting with spirit communication on their own. Divination tools that were once used for gaining wisdom and making predictions were now being used to speak to the dead. Divining methods that had once been reserved for mediums—such as automatic writing— became pastimes for the average person. New products like the Ouija board became a staple in the home.

People were beginning to realize that they could have meaningful conversations with spirits on their own.

It is this type of séance that you will be learning about in these pages. The steps for some of the divinatory tools and methods I have chosen for this book have not really changed since the height of spiritualism.

WHAT IS SPIRITUALISM AND WHO ARE THE SPIRITUALISTS?

Spiritualism began as a religious movement in the United States, most often inside different sects of Christianity.

Even today there are various registered religions around the world based on spiritualist beliefs and principles; however, not all people who identify as spiritualists are part of an established religion.

Generally, when I refer to spiritualists and spiritualism throughout this book, I am referring to **people in the nineteenth and early twentieth centuries who**

historically believed that communication could take place between the living and the dead.

Spiritualism was more than just a movement; it was an all-out craze. Some of the most influential people, like Thomas Edison, Mary Todd Lincoln, and Queen Victoria, participated.

There are three key reasons that spiritualism became a craze. If you remove any one of these factors, it is unlikely that spiritualism ever would have gained the momentum it did.

Key reason 01: Mass death

Death was a constant threat in the eighteenth, nineteenth, and early twentieth centuries. It was always lurking in the shadows, ready to snatch you up the moment you let your guard down.

The two biggest contributors to the high body count of the time were pandemics and war.

Pandemics

Between 1817 and 1923 there were multiple major cholera pandemics around the world. The first outbreak occurred in Russia, where cholera claimed over one million people. From there, the disease spread to the rest of Europe, and then on to Africa, North America, and Asia. In 1855, a vaccine was developed, but lack of access and hesitancy to use vaccines meant that outbreaks continued to proliferate.

Since cholera can kill in a span of just days or even hours, many of the bereaved didn't receive closure with their family members who perished.

War

The United States engaged in four major wars during the 1800s: the War of 1812, the Mexican-American War, the Civil War, and the Spanish-American War.

Indeed, the most notable contributor to spiritualism taking off in the United States was the Civil War, with four to six hundred people killed per day, totaling 750,000 dead by the time peace was declared.

The War of 1812 affected people from the United States, Canada, and Britain,

NOTICE

AT THE CONCLUSION OF THE

CABINET SEANCE

OF THE

DAVENPORT BROTHERS

MADAM ST. LAWRENCE

WILL GIVE WHAT IS TERMED A SPECIAL

"DARK SEANCE"

as well as the First Nations communities whose land was being co-opted by colonizers. Some of the earliest spiritualists may have been alive when these battles were taking place.

Spiritualism offered a way for grieving families to cope with the deaths of their loved ones as a result of these conflicts.

Key reason 02: Advertising

Advertising played a significant role in the lives of the American and British public between 1850 and 1920.

Advancements in both manufacturing and transportation led to more job opportunities, which led to more income for the average person.

For the first time, people had disposable income, as well as free time for leisure activities, such as séances.

By 1880, advertising had exploded in the West. Newspapers and department store catalogs were delivered to homes, while posters, flyers, and sandwich boards littered city streets.

If a business didn't engage in advertising, it was likely to go bankrupt.

Spiritualists and mediums began advertising as well.

Posters with ghostly images and catchy headlines like "PUBLIC SÉANCE—one night only! See the spectacular Davenport brothers" were tacked up in music halls, community centers, and grocery stores.

It is also believed that each week there was one book on spiritualism published, along with hundreds of periodicals and leaflets.

Spiritualists also made the conscious choice to advertise in women's spaces and women's magazines, which brings us to key reason number three for spiritualism's rise in popularity.

Key reason 03: Feminism

In the 1800s, spiritualism and feminism went hand in hand.

Spiritualism was one of the few places where women had not only a voice, but one that was respected.

Many men believed that women were more receptive to the spirits due to their assumed intuitive, sensitive natures and "weaker minds," so women were encouraged to take up mediumship.

Women, of course, saw this as a way in, and took full advantage of this opportunity to further their own agendas.

While working as mediums, women were able to spread messages and ideas to large groups of people all across the Americas and Europe. Not only did they have access to people, but their audiences were more receptive to hearing their ideas, due to the level of trust already at play within the situation.

For the first time, women were sitting alongside men and having theological discussions before heading off to do readings for presidents and queens.

Notably, the spiritual movement allowed Black women the opportunity to speak about key issues at a time when most public forums wouldn't allow their attendance, let alone their participation. In the United States, Black women hosted séances and lectures where they delivered messages against sexism and racism. Not only did people travel from far and wide to hear them speak; these women were also instrumental in creating safe spaces that centered the Black experience. Their audience was made up predominantly of Black women, but they did also hold lectures that white spiritualist women attended.

Unfortunately, as women began to gain power in the public sphere, many men who once supported them began resenting them.

Performing as mediums meant that women were taking back ownership of their personhood.

In spiritualism women had agency. They had agency over who their clients were, agency over their wages, and, most importantly, agency over who (or what) had access to their bodies and voices.

As spiritualism grew, men began investigating and debunking mediums. They saw themselves as the arbiters of logic and science, sent to suss out fake mediums taking advantage of people, and some men genuinely did help expose scams and tricks to unwitting consumers.

However, the way some of these "investigations" played out was horrifying.

Women under suspicion were often physically searched and patted down by groups of men. This was a time when modesty was something very central to the female experience, and it was taken from them because they dared to challenge the patriarchy.

Much ridicule and shaming of women in spiritual communities still exist today because women still make up the majority of people who identify as witches and hold New Age or occult beliefs. These spaces are also LGBTQA-friendly, as they challenge patriarchal ideas as well as toxic masculinity.

One striking example of this culturally accepted shaming is the abuse directed toward women who show an interest in Western astrology. Men who know nothing about astrology are quick to denounce it as fake, and its devotees as less intelligent.

Backlash against spiritualists wasn't just gendered; it was racist as well. Some spiritualists in the American South would cite séances as a reason to spread pro-slavery and anti-Black and anti-indigenous sentiments.

This backlash isn't unique to America either. In Europe, Romani people have faced centuries of abuse and persecution. Stereotypes relating to their use of divination have been employed to further this violence.

THE FOX SISTERS

Though spiritualism would not have taken off without these three key reasons, the general consensus in the paranormal community is that it was the Fox sisters who led to spirit communication becoming a sensation. The Fox sisters were to spiritualism what the Kardashians are to reality TV.

In March 1848, in Hydesville, New York, the Fox family was being plagued by knocking sounds that kept them up all through the night.

These knocks would echo through the house, and seemed to have no definitive source. They also appeared most active around the two youngest Fox girls: Margaretta, or Maggie, who was fourteen, and Kate, who was eleven.

Night after night, the girls would lie in bed and the knocking would begin. The family, who had searched the house repeatedly, even enlisting their neighbors to help, concluded that the knocks were the result of some otherworldly being. The girls began asking it questions.

"Count to five," they'd call out.

Rap...rap...rap...rap...rap...

"If you are an injured spirit, count three times."

Rap...rap...rap...

Eventually the family learned that the "spirit rappings," as they were called by one of the neighbors, belonged to the ghost of a peddler who had supposedly been robbed and murdered and then buried under the house by its former occupant.

Some sources say that after receiving this information, the family dug under the house and discovered hair and bone fragments; others say that groundwater began leaking into the basement, which stopped the investigation.

Regardless, word of the spirit disturbance spread like wildfire, and reached neighboring counties in days.

This is how the girls' older sister, Leah Fish (née Fox), learned about what was plaguing her siblings.

The girls promptly moved into her home, but the spirit rapping followed them.

It was then that Leah realized the girls were sitting on a gold mine.

The trio began hosting séances at home. The entrance fee was a dollar, and people were more than happy to pay to see the phenomenon.

As the girls' fame reached the rest of New York State and the surrounding area of New England, more and more families began coming forward with stories of their own rapping spirits.

For years, the girls were carted around and forced to perform for audiences. They were subjected to public scrutiny and private searches of their bodies and various experiments.

These traumas left the girls with mental health struggles and issues with substance abuse.

Forty years later, Maggie, who had developed a severe alcohol addiction, made a startling confession: she and her sister Kate had started the knockings as a prank.

Many people took issue with her confession, as she was in the throes of addiction and living in poverty, and the host of the event she spoke at had paid her a large sum of money.

The relationship between Leah and her younger sisters had also been fraught with turmoil, leading some to wonder if Maggie's confession had been aiming to wound her older sister.

Not only that, but Maggie had converted to Catholicism a few years prior, and there was pressure from the Catholic Church to denounce spiritualism.

And finally, Maggie herself recanted this confession just a year later.

Regardless of what you believe, it's obvious that these girls, who were of an age when they did not truly understand what was happening to them, were abused and taken advantage of by the very people who were supposed to have loved and protected them.

4

The Other Side

WHAT IS "THE OTHER SIDE" AND "THE AFTERLIFE"?

"The other side" is really just a catchall term for the place our spirit or soul goes when we die.

If you are part of a religion, you may know this place as heaven or paradise, or perhaps as something else. Feel free to substitute "the other side" with a word or phrase that aligns with your personal belief system.

For some people, the state of death is just a different state of consciousness. They believe that when our body dies, our stream of consciousness, our identity—whatever you want to call it—lives on. This act of living on is known as being in the afterlife. The afterlife can take place on the other side, or it can be in the same place that the living still reside, but on a different plane.

WHAT ARE THE PLANES?

In many branches of esotericism and in spiritualism, there is a strong belief that the other side consists of different realms or energetic places and frequencies known as "planes."

The three main planes are the physical plane, the astral plane, and the spiritual plane, though some groups believe there are as many planes as there are people!

The physical plane is the energetic level where you and I exist. It is our thoughts, our bodies, and the rest of the physical world that we interact with.

The astral plane, which is also known as the spirit realm, is the "in between" plane. We are thought to be able to access this plane while in different states of

consciousness, such as sleep, deep meditation, and death. Some believe this is where ghosts and other spirits exist, and therefore we are able to see and communicate with them because living people also have access to this plane.

The spiritual plane is a plane that consists of collective consciousness and ideas of divinity. It is where universal truths exist and are only accessed by the dead and highly spiritually evolved people.

For many people the astral plane and the spiritual plane are one and the same—you can decide what name feels right to you.

WHAT EXISTS ON THE OTHER SIDE?

There is no shortage of beings and spirits who exist on the other side. I have done my best to list the most common ones for you here.

Ghosts and spirits

The terms "ghosts" and "spirits" are often used interchangeably (this book is no exception!), but there is an important distinction to be made between them.

A spirit is the animating force that exists in all things, whether they are living, dead, or supernatural.

Your spirit is the thing that makes you you. In fact, you have likely heard people described by the state of their spirit, such as "He had a lively spirit" or "Her spirit was broken."

If you believe in an afterlife, you therefore must believe that your spirit continues on in some form after your physical body has died.

The term "soul" can be used interchangeably with "spirit." However, in some branches of Christianity, they are distinct from each other: the soul is your essence, and the spirit is the connection your soul has to God.

In this book, when I use the term "spirits," I am most often referring to people who once lived and are now dead.

A ghost, on the other hand, is the sensory manifestation of the spirit of a deceased person. Most often this physical manifestation refers to an appearance in a visual form, known as an apparition.

Hauntings are encounters with ghosts and spirits. These encounters are split into four main subgroups: intelligent, residual, psychokinetic, and nonhuman. (We'll cover these more extensively later in the chapter.)

Spirit guides and guardian angels

A spirit guide is an entity or divine being that exists on the other side and acts as a spiritual protector or mentor for a living human.

Spirit guides fall into two categories: human and nonhuman.

Human spirit guides are people who once lived and are now dead, but not all people who die become spirit guides. Most often, these guides are ancestors of the person they now watch over.

Nonhuman spirit guides are beings who never lived on the physical plane, though they may resemble humans. Angels are a type of spirit guide that many people of all faiths feel a connection to, and they fall into this category.

Both human and nonhuman spirit guides, sometimes just called guardian angels, are thought to be able to interact with events on the physical plane. Most often they are compelled to stop something bad from happening to their charge, such as being injured or killed. We have all heard stories about people who have walked away from horrific car crashes without a scratch and then claim they were "pulled out" before impact or protected in some way.

Demons

The concept of demons spans human existence. The idea that "lower vibrational beings" interfere with human lives and encourage wickedness is quite common.

Before the term "demon" became the antithesis to "angel," it actually meant any type of supernatural being—either good or bad. The word itself is derived from the Greek *daimon*, which simply means "spirit."

Not everyone believes in demons, but it is still a good idea to spiritually protect yourself if spirits or dark entities concern you. I talk more about setting spiritual boundaries on page 66.

Are demons something humans have created? It's possible. There is a theory known as conscious creation that is heavily debated in the paranormal community as well as in the witchcraft community. Conscious creation is the idea that if a person or group of people believe strongly in something, their energy can actually bring it into existence.

> *DISCLAIMER: If demons or evil spirits are major concerns, then spirit communication may not be right for you. Just as abusive people exist in life, they can also exist in death.*

Shadow people

Shadow people are a phenomenon experienced by people around the world. Often described as frightening, shadow people are exactly what their name suggests: dark, shadowlike human figures.

Shadow people were brought to the mainstream on the *Coast to Coast* radio show, when host Art Bell interviewed a First Nations elder and teacher named Harley SwiftDeer Reagan, who spoke of different legends about the phenomenon. Calls quickly flooded the station from people who had seen and interacted with these entities.

If you would like to explore shadow people further, there is an abundance of books available on the topic. Paranormal researcher Heidi Hollis was the first person to publish a book on the shadow people and was also a frequent guest on *Coast to Coast*, and paranormal heavyweight Mike Ricksecker has also written an in-depth guide on these mysterious beings.

Are shadow people evil? It's hard to say. Interactions range from positive to negative, but the majority seem to skew negative. At the very least, they are described as mischievous entities.

What are shadow people? These are the most common theories:

They are spirits who can't fully manifest as apparitions.

They are the spirits of those who were evil in life.

They are living people who are just astral traveling.

They are demonic entities.

They are aliens.

While shadow people can be seen anywhere, they do tend to frequent hospitals, prisons, asylums, and cemeteries. They also appear at people's bedsides in the middle of the night.

My personal belief is that a shadow person is an astral traveler, or perhaps a type of grim reaper figure out collecting souls who have passed in order to bring them to the other side. Sort of like a death tour guide or welcoming committee. Perhaps the state of sleep isn't always easy for them to discern from death, and that's why we wake up to them standing over us.

The Hat Man, a shadow person Heidi Hollis has covered in detail, is a shadow person who appears in stories time and time again.

He is the only shadow person described as wearing clothing. He dons a fedora or other type of brimmed hat, as well as a trench coat. Many people believe he is in charge of the others, or has some type of authority or special significance.

Cryptids

Cryptids are creatures whose existence has yet to be proven by current (and widely accepted) scientific methods of study. Cryptids have been seen by many people, but not by groups large enough to be considered a credible sample size.

The most well-known cryptids are Sasquatch (a.k.a. Bigfoot) and the Loch Ness Monster.

Cryptids can be categorized as either humanoid or animal, as well as supernatural or mystical.

Many people believe that some cryptids move between the physical plane and the astral plane, whereas other cryptids, such as Bigfoot, exist on the physical plane and are just very elusive.

Elemental spirits

The term "elemental spirit" covers a broad range of mythological creatures, such as fairies, imps, and other nature spirits. They are often associated with the four elements of matter: earth, air, fire, and water.

Other beings

There are other creatures and spirits who are thought to exist across the three different planes as well as different realities, and who don't always fit neatly into categories. Stories and folklore surrounding them can blend between cultures and change over time.

Doppelgängers

"Doppelgänger" is a German word that means "double walker" and is used to describe a being that is an exact copy of a still-living person.

The most common belief around seeing your doppelgänger is that you are destined to die relatively soon, but that isn't the only theory.

Doppelgängers could be astral travelers, time travelers, or people experiencing a phenomenon known as a time slip.

A time slip is a paranormal event in which someone suddenly experiences being in a different time period (most often the past) without knowing how they got there. Some time slips last only seconds, while others can last hours.

Orbs

Orbs are glowing balls of light that are believed to be the soul or spirit of a deceased person traveling around on the physical plane.

Photos and videos of orbs are what many paranormal investigators provide as proof of a haunting, but they should be taken with a grain of salt. More often than not, these orbs are just dust, debris, or lens flare.

However, people who have seen orbs in real life say they are a comforting presence that helps provide closure. Orbs are most associated with sudden or unexpected deaths.

TYPES OF HAUNTINGS

As I mentioned earlier, hauntings can be categorized into four main groups.

Intelligent hauntings

An intelligent haunting is the conscious interaction between a ghost or spirit and a living person. Sometimes this occurs in the form of an apparition, and other times it transpires through verbal communication or objects moving in response to specific questions.

Intelligent hauntings are the type called upon in séances and some of the other divination methods mentioned in this book.

I share my most impactful intelligent haunting experience in the cartomancy chapter on page 85, but intelligent hauntings are actually part of my daily life. For me, every time I pick up my tarot or oracle cards, I am signaling to my ancestors and guides that I am open to communicating.

While to many people in the paranormal community my daily interactions are not "proof" of an afterlife, it doesn't change the fact that for me, they are very real. What matters most about this work is your relationship with the spirits and what feels right to you.

Because cartomancy is part of my daily practice, I am very well versed in interpreting the messages I am being given via the images on the cards. Most of the time, these conversations (hauntings) are just general advice I need in order to go about my day, but I have also used these conversations to solve family mysteries.

A few short years ago, I was in the process of locating the graves of my ancestors who are buried close by. I had access to the cemetery sections and plot numbers for these relatives, but when it came to two of my great-great-grandparents, I was left a little stumped.

When I reached their assigned plot number, I could not find a stone anywhere within a twenty-foot radius. I couldn't find stones for anyone else in the vicinity either. I assumed they had been removed due to damage and would need to be replaced, but I still wanted to know where exactly their bodies were.

So I did what I always do in these situations: I took out my oracle deck that I had designed specifically for spirit communication and began to shuffle.

Now, I should note here that this deck contains over one hundred cards, which is quite a lot for my small hands. When two cards fell out of the deck and onto the ground, I didn't think much of it. That is, until I saw which cards they were.

Looking up at me from the grass were the images of a headstone and a shovel.

"You can't be serious," I said out loud to my great-great-grandparents. "I cannot just start digging without raising a million questions."

Generally, I do not recommend digging in a graveyard without permission. It can be illegal, depending on where you live. Always check with the caretaker's office, as well as local laws. Most cemeteries are fine with you planting flowers as long as you follow strict guidelines, but again, always, always, always ask permission.

That being said...I could not resist the urge to remove a bit of the grass with the toe of my boot.

Imagine my surprise when I caught a glimpse of granite just half an inch below where the cards had fallen. As I pulled back the rest of the dirt, the names Harvey and Eliza stared back at me.

As I stood on this large area of the cemetery that was completely covered in grass, my ancestors had guided me to this one-foot-by-one-foot spot and told me how to find them.

But the story doesn't end there.

After tidying the headstone (and asking maintenance to actually maintain the area), I felt I should ask the pair a few more questions.

As I shuffled, I asked them to tell me if they remembered their deaths. I received back two more cards: plague doctor and smoke.

Plague doctor represents an illness—that much is clear—but smoke was slightly more ambiguous...that is, until I thought about how smoke obstructs our breathing.

When I returned home, I decided to do some more research on my grandparents' cause of death. After a few hours I uncovered two death certificates.

Harvey and Eliza had died three weeks apart, due to pneumonia.

An illness that obstructs breathing.

Residual hauntings

A residual haunting is an energetic imprint on the environment left behind from an event. These hauntings are moments that happened in the past but are played out in the present, much like a scene in a movie. The actions happen in the same order every time.

The ghosts involved in residual hauntings are rarely, if ever, intelligent ghosts. Apparitions appear, act out their role, and then vanish. Sometimes there is no apparition—rather, just sounds or smells.

The cause of residual hauntings remains unclear. Some can be frightening and traumatic, while others involve mundane daily activities, like reading a newspaper or walking up stairs.

Many people believe that certain environments are capable of storing or recording energy, which later manifests as residual hauntings.

Certain types of stones or areas with an abundance of moisture are the main focus of these theories.

One famous residual haunting took place at the notorious Winchester Mystery House in San Jose, California.

In 1884, construction began on the house, which was owned by Sarah Winchester, the heiress to the Winchester rifle company, who was tormented by ghosts. The story goes that a psychic medium advised Sarah to build the house and to never stop adding odd and unusual rooms to it.

The idea behind this was that the ghosts would be tricked by all the hidden rooms and staircases leading to nowhere and would therefore leave the woman alone.

However, it wasn't one of these malicious spirits who got stuck at the Winchester house; no, it was a construction worker known as Clyde.

Clyde is still seen around the house in various places. Sometimes he is pushing a wheelbarrow in the basement, while other times he is spotted by the fireplace in the ballroom.

Other ghosts around the estate are considered to be of the intelligent variety because of their interactions with guests and visitors. Clyde does not interact and is clearly a residual haunting.

How long Clyde will remain at the house turned museum is anyone's guess.

Psychokinetic hauntings

Psychokinesis, or PK for short, is essentially a haunting by poltergeist.

Most people have heard the term "poltergeist," which means "noisy ghost" or "rumble ghost," but these types of hauntings are largely misunderstood due to television and movies.

PK hauntings are caused by the energy of a living person, rather than the energy of a spirit. Whether the living person—typically a girl in the beginnings of puberty—is the only source of the energy is unclear. It's possible that a spirit could be attracted by the emotions of the human agent, and then manipulate her.

PK hauntings are often very chaotic and involve moving objects and making noises, and are often connected to unstable or unhappy home environments. When these emotional issues are addressed, the activity typically ceases and things return to normal.

Nonhuman hauntings

Nonhuman hauntings are typically associated with negative or demonic energies. This is known as an infestation and can be very disruptive to daily life. However, not all nonhuman hauntings are negative.

A nonhuman entity is just that: not human. These hauntings can be the result of elementals, cryptids, and even angels.

> Both PK and nonhuman hauntings are also part of the intelligent category, but they are not the focus of this book.

Now that we have a clearer understanding of the other side, we need to understand our role and the special abilities we possess that allow us to communicate with spirits.

I am of the personal belief that we are all born with psychic and mediumship abilities. For most people, these abilities are skills that need to be practiced consistently, while others are naturally attuned to that frequency.

Either way, the potential for skills lies within us all, and can be strengthened to help us communicate with spirits. I have included some exercises for this purpose at the end of this chapter.

WHAT IS A PSYCHIC AND WHAT IS A MEDIUM?

When we think of psychics, we often picture those annoying pop-up ads on our favorite websites or a room full of telephone operators who charge $1.99 a minute to make "predictions" about our love life, but the reality is that we are all psychic and contain psychic abilities. As a creature of this earth and the physical plane, you are connected energetically to all other living things and all the energy that is contained in this world.

But what exactly does it mean to be psychic? Well, being psychic means you have the ability to gather information in ways outside the natural laws. This can be through telepathy or hearing others' thoughts, or perhaps you can predict the future and see visions of what is to come.

Being a medium or having mediumship abilities means you are capable of communicating with the spirits of the dead.

Though these terms are used interchangeably, not all psychics consider themselves mediums.

Both psychics and mediums use specific abilities in order to gather information, and the most well-known of these are the clairs. There are many types of clairs, but the three we will focus on are clairvoyance, clairaudience, and clairsentience.

Clairvoyance translates as clear seeing or psychic seeing.

For clairvoyants, messages from spirits can appear in many ways. For some they arrive as images or symbols in the mind, while others see full-bodied apparitions in real time on the physical plane.

Clairaudience translates as clear hearing or psychic hearing.

Clairaudients hear messages from spirits in the form of sounds, voices, and even music. For some, these sounds are disembodied and exist outside the mind, but for others, they exist in the mind as an inner dialogue. It's most comparable to reading a book: you hear the words in your own voice in your head, but those words don't belong to you or were not thought up by you.

Clairsentience translates as clear sensing or psychic sensing.

For clairsentients, messages from spirits come as feelings and sometimes thoughts. It is similar to clairaudience in that there is an internal knowing that the feelings and thoughts you are experiencing are not your own.

Clairsentience is like an enhanced form of intuition, something we all understand, but for someone with highly developed clairsentience, this internal knowing is much, much stronger.

Physical mediums

Mediums who rely on the clairs are known as mental mediums. The other type of mediumship is physical, which came into fashion during the spiritualism movement.

Because mediums were competing with one another for business, they needed to stand out in order to make money. During séances, they would employ any number of stage tricks and illusions in order to convince their audience that spirits were present.

One big way this was accomplished was by using a substance known as ectoplasm.

Paranormal ectoplasm, a term coined by paranormal researcher Charles Richet in 1894, is a physical substance created by mediums while in a trance or channeling.

This viscous material would exit from the mouths—and other orifices—of mediums at the height of their show. They claimed it was a spiritual "residue" of sorts.

The truth is, there is no substantial evidence that paranormal ectoplasm exists. These mediums were experts at faking this supposed spiritual matter. Many would even swallow materials like muslin, gauze, or cheesecloth and teach their bodies to regurgitate it effortlessly onstage.

In a way, it's a shame that mediums were forced to resort to these tricks, because physical mediumship is such a big part of divination, especially types like automatic writing and rhabdomancy.

It is my hope that with the help of this book, you will learn to work with your own mental and physical mediumship skills and create a fulfilling practice for communicating with the spirits.

EXERCISES

The following exercises are designed to help you increase your intuition and natural clair abilities.

When developing these abilities, the focus should be on consistency. The exercises I have created are simple enough to learn individually or in pairs and to be practiced a few times a week.

These practices are tailored to help you become more aware of your surroundings in your day-to-day life. Because we are constantly inundated with lights and sounds and other distractions, our intuition can get overstimulated, causing us to stop listening to it.

You may find that you are naturally inclined toward one skill in particular, but I urge you to work on them all.

Not only do these exercises increase your clair abilities; they also help you become better at divination.

Clairvoyance exercise 01

This first exercise focuses on external seeing.

1. At the start of the day, choose three objects from around your house. These can be anything, such as a teacup, a tube of toothpaste, or a plant.

2. Take a mental snapshot of each object. Notice each one's color and texture. Do you remember how you procured each item?

3. Then, throughout your day, whether you are working or running errands, see how many times you come across versions of these same objects.

4. Make note of the similarities between the ones you encounter and the ones you have at home.

In what context or situation did you encounter them?
How do they differ?
How are they the same?
What colors are they?
How old do you think they are?
If the objects were connected to a person, describe that person.

While this exercise is simple, you may find that it actually takes quite a bit of effort to get started. I recommend keeping a notebook for recording all the objects and descriptions. After a few weeks, take a look through and see how your process has evolved.

Clairvoyance exercise 02

This second exercise focuses on internal seeing.

1. Make a list of five to ten people. These can be family, friends, or even celebrities.

2. Next, close your eyes and take a few breaths.

3. Visualize each person one by one. Where are they? What color are they wearing? What hairstyle do they have?

4. Next, ask to be shown an object that symbolizes each person. Your personal biases and opinions may bleed into these symbols, and that is perfectly fine. Allow this to happen.

5. Write down the symbols for each person and any impressions you got.

Were the symbols clear and straightforward?
Were some unexpected?

Example: After picturing your uncle George, you see a horseshoe. This can mean he is someone who is very lucky in life.

Use the tasseography dictionary (page 204) or the charm casting dictionary (page 247) to help you interpret the meanings for each symbol.

Clairaudience exercise 01

This first exercise focuses on external hearing.

1. At the start of the day, pick one song to listen to.

2. You can go with a longtime favorite or allow your streaming service to choose something at random.

3. I recommend wearing headphones so you can be fully immersed in the sounds.

4. Take a few breaths, press play, and close your eyes.

5. As you listen, notice how the music is making you feel.

6. Next, you will want to choose three words.

These words should be picked intuitively rather than just chosen at random. You should feel them jump out at you.

When you have your words, carry them with you throughout the day. Take note of anywhere they come up. This could be on billboards, in conversations, or even in other songs.

Clairaudience exercise 02

This second exercise focuses on internal hearing and spirit guides or spirit communication. You will need the help of a partner.

1. Gather five mugs or teacups (a clear glass will not work), five napkins, and two coins. The coins can be of any denomination, and to make this challenge harder, you can make them both different denominations.

2. Next, ask your helper to put the two coins in two of the cups and to cover all five cups with a napkin.

3. Take a few moments to breathe and center yourself.

4. When you feel ready inside your mind, ask your guide or spirit of choice to tell you where each of the coins is.

Take your time with this. The answer may be heard in your own voice or as a voice separate from yourself.

Before you check the cups, record the answers you received, as well as any emotions that came up during the process. When you're ready, check where the coins are actually located. Were you right? Make a note of the results.

It's okay if you don't receive an answer right away; just keep trying. As time goes on you can increase the difficulty of this exercise by bringing more cups into the mix.

Clairsentience exercise 01

This first exercise focuses on external feeling.

For this exercise, you will be focusing on a practice known as psychometry. Psychometry is the act of receiving psychic messages or feelings from inanimate objects.

1. The first thing you need to do is head to your local thrift or antique store with the intention of picking two or three small objects.

2. Take your time browsing, and make a mental note of what items you are drawn toward. It's okay to let personal taste influence your decision, but it should not be the main focus.

3. Decide on your pieces, purchase them, and bring them home.

4. When you're home, let the objects settle into the space for a few days.

5. After you're all acclimatized to one another's presence, you can begin the second part of this exercise.

6. Place the objects in front of you and look at each one. How do they make you feel? Write down your initial reaction.

7. Next, hold each one for a few moments, and once again write down how you feel. This could be summed up in one word, or an object could spark a blend of many different emotions that require more detail.

Clairsentience exercise 02

This last exercise focuses on internal feeling.

The purpose of this exercise is to help you get more in touch with your own emotions.

When we are in tune with our feelings, we are better able to differentiate psychic emotions from the feelings of others.

Over the next month, take some time throughout each day to write down how you are feeling. I like to break this up into morning, noon, and night. At the end of the day, I look at what I've written for these three periods and compare them.

You Are Invited

Dearest _____

Your spiritual presence is kindly requested to participate in all
current and future Seances hosted by _____

5

How to Perform a Séance

WHY HOLD A SÉANCE?

We all talk to ghosts.

When we need advice, we silently wish our father was still here to help.

Or when we are alone and hear a strange noise, we ask from underneath our covers, "Is someone there?"

The fact of the matter is, the dead are a much bigger part of our lives than many of us realize. The problem is, we don't always know how to listen for a response, or when we do get one, we aren't sure how to interpret it.

The reasons for wanting to communicate with spirits are highly personal. Perhaps you need advice about a certain situation or need help resolving a family conflict. It could even be just because you are curious to see if it works.

I recommend writing out your reasons on a piece of paper that you keep somewhere safe so you can review it along your spirit communication journey. It may stay the same, or it may evolve.

PERSONAL RECOMMENDATION

Though many types of spirits exist, I recommend communicating only with family and friends who have passed on. When I mention spirits throughout this book, those are the ones I am referring to.

I also recommend holding off on spirit communication if you are in the early stages of mourning or in a period of emotional instability.

Using divination to communicate with the other side is pretty safe. Despite what Hollywood would have you believe, dark forces aren't lurking around every corner, looking to hurt you. Of course, this doesn't mean you should skip protecting yourself; do not foster relationships with spirits who feel abusive or negative in nature.

OUTLINE YOUR BOUNDARIES

The first and most important way to protect yourself while contacting spirits is by establishing your personal boundaries.

In the same way we have boundaries for the living, we also need them for the dead. You wouldn't let strangers walk into your house in the middle of the night, or jump into your car when you're stopped at a red light, would you? Of course not! By establishing clear boundaries before you begin a séance, you are protecting your energy, time, and personal space.

REMEMBER: Spirit communication should be fun! You should walk away from a séance feeling positive.

Spend a few weeks or months working through the following steps. It can be tempting to begin spirit communication right away, but it is better to wait until you feel comfortable and confident.

Step 1: Decide what is right for you.
Some people are okay with spirits visiting often or without an invitation; other people are not.

Just because you want to communicate with spirits, it doesn't mean you have to accept anyone who comes to the door. If you had a rocky relationship with your grandmother Marian while she was alive, it is more than okay to tell her she is not welcome at your sessions.

I recommend saying out loud what your intentions are, and who you would like to communicate with. Begin by calling for one specific person until you feel comfortable.

You can also take this a step further and write invitations to the spirits you'd like to attend. Keep these in a safe place, preferably with some family heirlooms or photographs.

Step 2: Show up for the spirit.
If you want spirits to be consistent with you, you need to be consistent with them. Before your first séance, I recommend establishing a daily ritual for bonding with the spirits. This can be burning incense, lighting a candle, meditating, or even pouring an extra cup of coffee in the morning as an offering. I recommend performing this ritual at the same time every day to help build trust.

I have an ancestor altar next to my computer, and every single morning I light a white candle. While it burns, I speak to my family members about my day, or steps I have been taking to honor their legacy. Spirits have free will too, and don't appreciate being called on only when you need something. This relationship should be a mutual give-and-take.

Step 3: Grab a good luck charm.
Amulets have been used for thousands of years to protect people from bad luck and "unseen" forces. Whether you believe amulets have magical powers or not,

you can hopefully agree that they do shift your mood in a more positive direction.

For some of you, this could mean carrying a rosary. For others, it could mean putting on your lucky underwear. Personalize it.

Step 4: Get in a good mindset.

Before any séance, you will want to evaluate your mood. If you are angry, scared, in distress, or under the influence in any way, wait until another time.

You should feel positive, clearheaded, and relaxed.

Many people turn to spirit communication to deal with grief, but I recommend waiting until you have processed a loss before attempting to communicate.

If you suffer from mental health issues, paranoia, or delusions of any kind, séances are not right for you.

When in doubt, seek out a licensed therapist or mental health professional.

Step 5: Don't go looking for trouble.

This should go without saying, but don't attempt to communicate with murderers and other abusive people. I don't recommend going to locations that are believed to have dark entities.

Paranormal investigators take on these people quite regularly, but they know what to look out for and they prepare for any potential risks or fallout.

Being scared is fun for an afternoon, but it's a different story when you can't sleep at night for a month.

Step 6: Try protective visualization.

If you are a visual person, you may find it helpful to perform a "protective bubble" or psychic shield ritual.

This is as simple as envisioning a protective ball of golden light surrounding you that nothing harmful can penetrate.

SACRED SPACES

What is a sacred space?

A sacred space is a place that humans have designated to have spiritual or religious significance.

Churches, temples, and cemeteries are all examples of sacred spaces. Many were built at sacred natural sites, created in such harmony with their environments as to render them not just practical but divine.

For instance, in County Meath, Ireland, stands an impressive prehistoric monument called Newgrange.

This passage tomb has a small window carved into the stone above the entrance known as a roof box. At dawn on the winter solstice, a ray of sunshine enters through this opening and illuminates the tomb. The sun has always been sacred, and this feat of engineering goes to show just how much reverence the ancient Neolithic people put into their spiritual practice.

Natural beauty can also be used as an energetic tether. Ponds and rivers, forests and groves, and even flower fields can all be utilized for protection and spirit communication.

In 1921, a well-known landscape photographer, inventor, and amateur archaeologist named Alfred Watkins began to develop his own theory that the sacred monuments and environmental wonders around his home of Herefordshire, England, were connected by metaphysical energy lines he called leys. In some cases, he even photographed impressions on the earth that he said showed these lines. These routes were used for centuries to connect people with their community, and walking these trails and paths yourself may help foster a connection to all the people who journeyed there before.

Though their existence has been hotly debated, both then and now, searching for ley lines around Britain and the rest of the world has become a pastime for many people. The UK and Ireland are littered with remnants of sacred stone circles, old churches, and monuments that, whether you believe in ley lines or not, were placed there because of their spiritual significance.

Choosing a sacred space

You can perform your séance in one of these spiritual or culturally significant areas. There are pros and cons for each.

Churches and temples

PROS

- If you have a cultural or religious affiliation to a place, that gives you an easy energetic link to it. Perhaps growing up, your grandfather brought you to church every Sunday, and you cherish those memories. These feelings can be incredibly spiritually impactful on the environment and on your interpretation of messages.
- Houses of worship are specifically designed to be both protective and spiritual. Therefore, many people feel safe and calm when inside them.
- In Europe, many Christian churches were built on top of or near sacred monuments from civilizations past, providing thousands of years of history to connect to.

CONS

- Obtaining permission to access these buildings can be difficult, especially if you want to do something that isn't necessarily supported by the organization. Always be respectful in your requests and never lie to get what you want.
- Séances can be offensive to some religious groups. Just because you feel comfortable communicating with spirits or using certain tools doesn't mean that everyone else has to be. Visitors and even some ghosts may be offended by what you are doing, especially if it goes against their beliefs.

Cemeteries or graveyards

I do want to mention that the use of cemeteries for séances and paranormal investigations is a subject of ongoing debate in the paranormal community. Use your own discretion. Personally, I am all for cemetery work. Be sure to always follow rules and safety guidelines outlined by the cemetery owner. Uneven ground and falling headstones can be deadly.

PROS

- Cemeteries can be wonderful places to visit and to perform a séance. They are often peaceful, well maintained, and incredibly powerful. If your goal is to communicate with the dead, it makes sense to head directly to the source.
- If you have ancestors or mentors buried in a cemetery, it is a great place to go to speak with them. Headstones are incredibly sacred and personal, and energy can be drawn from them by both you and the spirit.

CONS

- While you may not be bothered, you could accidentally be bothering someone else. There could be people actively mourning a recent death, and you may offend them inadvertently.

- You may feel self-conscious or judged. As much as spirit communication, witchcraft, and paranormal investigating have come into the mainstream, there are still a lot of people who don't understand and may cause problems for you.
- Most importantly, you could end up speaking to a spirit whom you have no intention of communicating with, especially if you haven't made your boundaries clear. While this isn't necessarily always bad, it can be unnerving for beginners.

Parks, forests, and other natural areas

PROS
- Parks and other green spaces are easily accessible to many people. In most cities, you at least have access to a public park.
- Nature is energetically soothing and inspiring, which encourages a positive mindset.
- There could be strong mythical or folkloric connections to an area that can be harnessed during your séance.

CONS
- Unless you have access to a private or secluded area, you run the risk of being disturbed during your séance.
- For people with mobility issues, some areas may be out of reach, or tiring to get to.
- Weather can change or animals can appear unexpectedly and cut your session short.

Creating a sacred space
The most obvious place to hold a séance is in the safety of your own home. Here you can create your very own sacred space for divination. It can be as simple as placing a candle on your coffee table or as elaborate as building shrines like the ones you see in temples.

There are many benefits to doing your séance at home, the most important being your comfort level. At home you are generally more relaxed, which will allow you to better interpret messages.

> Some people are nervous about inviting spirits into their home, which is why it is vital to set strong boundaries when you begin any sort of spirit communication (see page 66).

There are two main types of sacred spaces you can create: permanent and temporary.

Permanent sacred space

- This is a designated area that you use for communicating with spirits. A good example is an ancestor altar. This is a shrine to your family members who have passed on, and it contains objects, photographs, and other things of importance that once belonged to them.
- A permanent space is great for setting up ground rules and boundaries. If you are seated at the space, spirits know it is an appropriate time to stop by or communicate with you. When you are away from it, they know you are not interested in their presence just then.
- Having a permanent space is a good reminder to stay consistent with your divination, and it's also excellent for building long-term relationships with spirits.

Temporary sacred space

- If you have a roommate or live with a partner, they may not want to have altars around the house at all times, so these sacred spaces can be set up when you actively need them.
- You may want to keep things private; having a space you can pack up heads off people asking you questions or touching your things.

- If physical space is an issue, temporarily setting up on a kitchen table or bureau means having that space available the rest of the time.

Placing objects and decorations in your sacred space is a great way to add not only protective layers of energy but also spiritual ones.

LAYERING

There are two analogies I like to use to explain the idea of layering.

Analogy 01: Home protection theory

If you want to protect your home and yourself, you lock your door. This will effectively deter most intruders, but not all of them. How can you improve the protection? Add an alarm system. Now you have two layers of protection. Want to go even further? Perhaps get a dog. You see where I am going with this?

Analogy 02: Aunt Dorothy theory

Let's say you're sitting down to do an automatic writing session, and you want to communicate with your great-aunt Dorothy. Well, having her cherished necklace in the space is definitely going to attract her. Adding her favorite flowers to the mix shows her the effort you're making to be close to her. And if you cooked her secret family recipe earlier in the day, well, you may end up with a permanent spectral houseguest.

Layering items

Candles

Candles are a mainstay in almost all spiritual and religious practices. In many cases they represent the life force or soul of various gods and deities. Not only are candles affordable; they are easy to procure. In a séance, candles are symbolic of spiritual seeing, passion, warmth, and safety.

In some paths of witchcraft, like Wicca, candle color plays an important role in ritual, and can be incorporated into your séance (even if you aren't a witch).

These colors' meanings can also be applied to cloth and decorative objects!

Black: The dead, ancestors, protection, banishing

White: Spirit guides, healing, serenity, meditation

Red: Passion, love, sex, anger

Orange: Success, optimism, intellect, creativity

Yellow: Confidence, joy, childhood, manifestation

Green: Fertility, health and healing, money, career

Blue: Calm, peace, mourning, forgiveness

Purple: Psychic abilities, wisdom, divination, power

Pink: Love, beauty, romance, friendship

Brown: Stability, grounding, concentration, connection to animals

Gold: Wealth, fame, abundance, solar energy

Silver: Mystery, subconscious, balance, lunar energy

Incense and plants

Like candles, incense is used all around the world for religious ceremonies, as well as for aromatherapy. When most people think of incense, they picture the resin sticks that were invented in India. These sticks come in a variety of scents, as well as price points, which makes them accessible to most people.

If you aren't able to use smoke in your home, you can keep herbs, flowers, and other plants in your space in order to draw upon their energy. These can be dried or living; it is a matter of personal preference.

Please do not ingest anything unless you are certain it is safe to do so. I also do not recommend performing a séance intoxicated or under the influence in any way.

Cedar: Purification, psychic powers, success

Frankincense: Psychic protection, strength, perseverance

Rosemary: Home protection, spiritual cleansing, creativity, sensitivity

Pine: General protection, healing, longevity

Cinnamon: Love, passion, power, career
Rose: Love, beauty, compassion, innocence
Clove: Remove negativity, restore balance, money
Lavender: Relaxation, serenity, happiness, dreams
Patchouli: Focus, meditation, cleansing, balance
Sandalwood: General protection, persistence, purification, spiritual cleansing
Lemongrass: Remove negativity, mental clarity, focus, admiration
Juniper: Remove hexes, home and spiritual protection
Vanilla: Love, friendship, family, ancestors
Lily: Mourning, forgiveness, tranquility

Remember: With any incense or color, personal taste and emotional connection should take precedence over prescribed meaning.

Example: If your mom used to bake rosemary focaccia on Sunday afternoons, the scent of rosemary may conjure feelings of closeness and love.

Try writing down some of your own examples of scents that evoke memories!

Personal objects
Of course, the most important things to add to your sacred space are personal objects, especially if you are communicating with a specific person.

This is not a complete list, but it's a good place to begin: favorite foods and drinks, toys, games, photographs, jewelry and other heirlooms, letters and postcards, ashes, and funeral memorabilia.

Astrological forecasts
Astrology is one of the oldest and most popular methods of divination. The energy of astrological associations and phases of the moon can be drawn upon to enhance your séance in the same way that protective layers do.

Moon phases
The phases of the moon can be drawn upon to enhance your readings.

NEW The new moon is all about beginnings and fresh starts. This is the best time to embark on a new spiritual practice.

WAXING MOON As the moon grows, so does the energy that surrounds us. The waxing moon expands our hearts and minds, which allows us to be more receptive to messages.

FULL MOON The full moon illuminates everything hidden in the shadows. This phase can be utilized for fast and intense results.

WANING MOON As the light of the moon diminishes, so do our fears and resentments. The waning moon is a great time for releasing grief.

Days of the week

The days of the week are another easy way to incorporate the energy of the universe into your séance. Each day is ruled by a different planet and has a specific focus.

MONDAY Ruled by the moon, Monday is a great day to work on matters relating to emotions, the past, and ancestral healing.

TUESDAY Tuesday is when the planet of war, Mars, takes the reins. For your readings, focus on protection, goal setting, and situations that require determination.

WEDNESDAY Wednesday is the perfect day to try spirit communication, as it is ruled by the planet of communication, Mercury.

THURSDAY Career and money matters are best explored on Thursday, as that is when Jupiter, the planet of expansion, brings positivity and luck to the week.

FRIDAY Friday is ruled by Venus, so this is the perfect time to work on matters relating to love and partnerships.

SATURDAY Saturday, or Saturn's day, is all about karmic healing, discipline, and forming lasting bonds. This is a great day to explore spirit work, as you will have a boost in protection from the planet.

SUNDAY The sun is inviting, warm, and positive; therefore, Sunday is a wonderful day for any type of divination you want to try.

KEEPING RECORDS

Keeping records is arguably the most important part of your séance. Nothing is worse than having a great session but forgetting to write down the details, or thinking you heard a spirit knocking, only to find out your neighbor was doing home repairs.

There will also be times when you receive a message that doesn't make sense in the moment, but clicks into place when you review it later. Beginners may find this to be true more often than not, so keeping notes is even more imperative if you're just starting out.

Records also reveal patterns over time, which can help us identify specific spirits, build our confidence when interpreting messages, and help us create our own meanings for symbols.

Records checklist

In each chapter in Part Two, you will find worksheets tailored to the specific divinatory methods you're using, but the following checklist should be utilized for every session.

- Date and time
- Participants
- Location
- Method of divination
- Astrological forecast
- Temperature and weather

- External factors (AC, fans, construction)
- Protective elements and layers used (incense, candles, etc.)

ALONE OR WITH A FRIEND?

As you learned in chapter 3, séances were historically performed by a medium, with a group of people present. While you can hold your séance with others, I highly recommend doing it alone.

There are multiple reasons for this:

- You won't need to divert energy from the séance into regulating other people's emotions or fears.
- You can release your inhibitions and ask about private or personal matters.
- You won't need to worry about someone else skewing the results or playing tricks.
- You won't feel hurt if nobody shows up for you but someone shows up for them.
- You can take your time and personalize the session.

THE SÉANCE

You've focused your energy on the other side with a daily routine and decided which type of divination you'd like to use. Now it is time for the séance to begin.

The séance is, in a way, the easiest part of the entire process. It's everything you do leading up to it that establishes your connection to the spirits.

Remember: This is the fun part!

Opening a session

Begin by preparing your divinatory tool, gathering your heirlooms, and setting up your sacred space. Do your best to remain calm and relaxed, but it's also okay to feel a little bit excited or nervous.

Take deep breaths and focus your intention. Think about the spirits you would like to communicate with and invite them to join you.

Knocking three times on your table or work surface is an easy and effective way to "wake up" the spirits.

When you feel ready, begin your chosen divination. Each one in this book has instructions that you should refer back to throughout your session as often as you need to. *I find it helpful to place a sticky note on the relevant pages so I can flip back and forth easily.*

Be methodical while asking your questions, and take your time. You should also take breaks throughout the session to write notes or collect your thoughts.

Closing a session

When you have finished all your questions and taken your notes, you can end the séance.

Thank the spirits for joining you and for their messages. Depending on your personal boundaries (page 66), you can then ask them to leave.

If you included a candle or incense in the séance, you can now snuff it out. This is a good way to signal that the session is closed and that visitors should depart.

Remember to cleanse your tools and store them correctly. You can find the instructions starting on page 280.

Don't be discouraged if you don't receive any coherent messages the first time, or if the answers you do receive aren't what you were expecting. It doesn't mean you were unsuccessful; you may just need to look at them again at a different time. I recommend devoting one afternoon a month to going through your notes and looking for patterns.

PART TWO

6

Cartomancy

WHAT IS CARTOMANCY?

Cartomancy is the art of interpreting or divining messages from a set of cards. Most often, this is done with a specific type of deck known as tarot cards.

Due to the abundance of tarot decks and books available, it is the best form of divination to begin with. There are sets for every budget and artistic taste imaginable. Because tarot meanings stay relatively uniform across the board, once you are familiar with them, you can use any deck.

The tarot consists of seventy-eight cards and is broken into two main categories known as the Major Arcana and the Minor Arcana. Both contain themes ranging from love to career to spirituality, but they speak to different orders of magnitude within a person's life.

The Major Arcana are the first twenty-two cards of the tarot and are numbered from zero to twenty-one. They depict the soul's journey and are archetypal in nature. They represent the big life events that every human experiences. The spiritual weight of these cards means that they are almost always made a priority in the context of a reading.

The Minor Arcana consist of the remaining fifty-six cards in the deck and are divided into four suits. Each suit is ruled by one of the four main elements (earth, air, fire, and water), and each is numbered ace through ten. Each suit also contains four named characters known as the court cards.

The Minor Arcana represent the smaller actions, scenarios, and events that we all encounter on a daily basis.

HOW DOES TAROT WORK FOR SPIRIT COMMUNICATION?

Cartomancy is a perfect blend of the three divination types we covered in chapter 2. Shuffling and drawing cards is a form of casting; viewing the images and symbols on the cards is a form of scrying; and interpreting the message revealed by the spirits is a form of channeling.

Humans have been using symbolism to communicate different ideas for millennia. Tarot is just a collection of these symbols. You can find any scenario imaginable illustrated among the cards—which is why spirits love to communicate through them. Even if the spirits in question have no prior knowledge of the meanings, they can still craft a compelling story for their audience using the images as an alphabet of sorts.

HISTORY

Despite the ever-growing community of tarot readers and the massive increase in tarot decks created in the last few decades, a lot of misinformation surrounds these seventy-eight cards. In fact, many people typically mistake them for having magical or supernatural origins.

The truth is, tarot was created as a parlor card game in Italy in the fifteenth century.

Over the following centuries, some cards were added, others were removed, and what was once just a fun pastime became forever intertwined with mysticism and the occult, thanks to a man named Jean-Baptiste Alliette.

In the eighteenth century, playing cards of all types were introduced into divination, and Jean-Baptiste, who was better known by the pseudonym Etteilla, decided to commission his own deck specifically designed for fortune-telling. In fact, he is credited with creating the word "cartonomancie," which has since evolved into today's "cartomancy."

The Etteilla Tarot is the first time we see references to the elements, numerology, and astrology appear in the tarot.

While this would become known as the turning point for cartomancy, in his lifetime, Etteilla was looked upon with skepticism for his lack of formal education. Because he dedicated his life to studying and writing about tarot, he thankfully had a loyal group of followers who continued his work after he was gone and preserved the memory of the first mainstream tarot reader.

In 1909, the tarot would once again go through a reinvention, with the creation of the Rider-Waite deck (now also known as the Waite-Smith deck), the version still used today.

Arthur Edward Waite was born in 1857 in Brooklyn, New York, and brought to England by his mother when he was just a boy, after his father's untimely death. As he grew up, Arthur showed an interest in writing and history, and eventually his focus narrowed to the study of the occult and magic.

In 1891, he joined the Hermetic Order of the Golden Dawn, a secret society that was devoted to the study of mysticism and the paranormal. He would leave the order just a few years later, only to rejoin various offshoots of the organization over the years, eventually creating his own.

During this time, a young artist named Pamela Colman Smith, who was also known as Pixie, was working as an illustrator and designer for a theater company. Here she ran with a tight group of influential friends, one of whom was author Bram Stoker.

Pixie had always been interested in the bohemian scene and alternative arts, and before long, her friend the poet William Butler Yeats, who was himself big into the occult, introduced her to the Hermetic Order of the Golden Dawn, where she met the infamous Arthur Waite.

Together, Arthur and Pixie began their journey into the world of the tarot.

Arthur conceptualized the deck while Pixie illustrated. They expanded the size of the deck into the seventy-eight-card version we use today. Not only that, but they broke away from the traditional pip art style, with Pixie creating elaborately illustrated scenes for all the Minor Arcana.

Arthur died in 1942, leaving behind a vast collection of occult texts and poetry. It is unknown if he and Pixie remained in contact during those later years, but it can be assumed that he was the only one who benefited from the tarot monetarily.

Unfortunately, despite her success and popularity in her early life, Pixie was never able to capitalize on this momentum and died in poverty in her small apartment in September 1951. It is believed she is buried in an unmarked grave in St. Michael's Cemetery, which is no longer in use.

In 1971, the company U.S. Games bought the rights to the deck, and forever changed the landscape of cartomancy, throwing both Pixie and Arthur posthumously into the spotlight.

I can only hope that wherever she is now, Pixie knows how valued she is.

PARANORMAL STORY

In the spring of 2016, a close family friend, whom I will call James, went missing while visiting a relative at the relative's home, located on the shores of Lake Huron, in Ontario. James grew up there, so he knew the area very well.

After learning that he had gone missing, I decided to turn to the tool I know best to try and get answers: the tarot.

The search party and police theorized that he had taken a bus out of town, but my family immediately suspected the worst: that he had drowned.

A few weeks prior to going missing, James had expressed interest in getting a tarot reading from me. He liked a morbidly hilarious deck of mine that features zombies behaving like living people. James was the epitome of the class clown, so this deck really spoke to his personality and sense of humor. When he went missing, I decided to use that deck for guidance about his possible location and to help calm my mind.

I asked out loud for a sign from him about where he might be, and while I was still shuffling, I received my answer.

The King of Cups fell out of the deck and landed faceup on my coffee table.

The traditional meaning of this card is an emotionally intelligent and light-hearted person. While that described James as I knew him, it was actually the illustration on the card that told me what I needed to know.

A zombie face smiled back at me, sitting upon a throne underwater.

Now, for a lot of people, that would be a jarring way to learn that someone you love has indeed drowned. But if you knew James, you'd understand how special that moment was between us.

I was devastated when his body was recovered from the lake two months later, but it has been comforting to know that whenever I pick up that particular deck, I am close to him.

CHOOSING A DECK

There are two main schools of thought when it comes to choosing your tarot deck. Both are equally valid, and it really comes down to personal preference.

Option A: Buy the Rider-Waite deck.

As we learned, this is the most popular tarot deck in the world, and the basis for the majority of other deck designs and card meanings.

PROS

- **Affordable and accessible:** This deck is very easy to find in stores and online, and it fits most budgets.
- **Stylized scenes:** Its highly illustrated scenes featuring lots of people and symbols make this deck very beginner-friendly.
- **Lots of resources:** There is an abundance of information about this deck online and in books.

CONS

- **Lack of diversity:** There is little to no racial or gender diversity in this deck.
- **Personal taste:** You may find that you do not connect with the art style.

Option B: Choose your own deck.

It is most common to choose your deck based on personal preference and taste; this can help build your energetic connection to the cards.

PROS

- **Personal taste:** There is an amazing spectrum of themed decks and themed art styles to choose from these days. You can find anything from TV-show-inspired decks to animal decks and even decks designed specifically for spirit communication!
- **Card stock:** You can experiment with different card stock thicknesses and finishes, like matte and gloss. Some stores even have dedicated display decks, which are great for testing how the cards shuffle or fit in your hands.
- **Diversity:** Modern decks have lots of diversity and feature people from all walks of life. It can help build a connection to the deck if you see yourself and your loved ones represented.
- **Support artists:** You can support local artists by purchasing their self-published decks, which often encourages big publishers to take them on as clients.

CONS

- **Difficulty:** Sometimes you are drawn to the look of a deck but find it isn't very beginner-friendly when you use it.
- **Price:** Indie decks come in a wide range of prices, and sometimes they can be prohibitively expensive.
- **Discontinued:** Nothing feels worse than falling in love with a deck only to find out when you need to replace it that it has been discontinued or retired.

TAROT MYTHS

Too often when someone begins looking into cartomancy, they become discouraged by the myths and rumors that follow the practice.

I feel it is important to clarify—and in some cases even dispel—these persistent ideas.

Myth 1: Your first tarot deck must be gifted to you.

False.

Anyone can buy any deck, at any time. What matters is how you feel about it, and the emotional connection you develop over time with the deck.

Myth 2: The Death card means you will die.

False (mostly).

For starters, we all die. It's an unfortunate fact of life.

Before you panic, understand that this card predominantly speaks of metaphorical or symbolic death. Think relationships ending, seasons changing, or other "life cycles" that have a natural end.

Yes, it can reference physical death, especially if you are using tarot to communicate with spirits. But it is extremely unlikely that the card is foretelling your own death.

Myth 3: Tarot cards are magical.

False…ish.

The main use of tarot cards is to get insight into your own psyche in order to solve problems. The patterns we see in the cards reflect the self and the unconscious thought patterns all humans have.

However, some people, like me, believe that spirit guides and ghosts can use the deck to relay messages to us.

Myth 4: Tarot cards are evil.

False.

Tarot cards contain vast symbology and ideas that can be classed as both positive and negative. What we do with that energy is what matters most. Fears surrounding tarot are often the product of religious ideology and indoctrination. Many people who grow up with a heavy religious influence are taught to fear tarot based on misinformation. These days, though, many religious people are adopting tarot reading for themselves and see it as a sacred connection to God.

READING THE CARDS

> A NOTE ON GENDER: The tarot contains many named characters that often reflect the outdated gender binary. I have used she/her, he/him, and they/them pronouns throughout my dictionary, but pronouns can be interchanged wherever you feel it's appropriate. Despite the court cards having gendered titles, I have opted to use only they/them in their descriptions.

The tarot is traditionally read using configurations known as spreads. Spreads are made up of predetermined positions where you lay (place) a predetermined number of cards after thoroughly shuffling the deck. Each position represents a question or idea that is in alignment with the overall situation or reason for the reading.

Spreads can be as simple as one card, or as complex as all seventy-eight cards. There are spreads for every situation and scenario imaginable. I have provided you with some basic spreads for learning to read the cards, and two spreads designed specifically for spirit communication.

Some people do not use spreads and choose the number of cards they will read intuitively. This style of reading relies heavily on instinct and the ability to connect the cards in a way that tells a story.

Shuffling

Begin by shuffling your cards. Use this time to think of your question or focus on the spirit you'd like to contact.

Most people do what is known as overhand shuffling, holding the cards in one hand and using your other hand to move cards from the back of the deck to the front at random, but you can shuffle however feels right for you. What matters is that the cards are thoroughly mixed up, and that you cannot see their faces.

Drawing

Next, you will pull the number of cards your chosen spread calls for out of the deck and lay each one faceup in its designated position. It is easiest to take the cards from the top of the deck, but realistically they can come from anywhere.

The steps to reading the cards are the same whether you are reading for yourself or for someone else. The only difference is that in a reading, you may opt for the querent to shuffle or draw the cards themselves.

Reading

Now comes the fun part: interpreting the messages.

Take your time with this and start making notes. Use the sample worksheet on pages 99–100 to get started.

Are there repeating numbers or suits?
What about symbols or colors?
Is one element predominant? Are any missing?
Are there a lot of Major Arcana cards or none at all?

One-card spread

The one-card spread is exactly how it sounds. You think of a question and pull one card for your answer.

Three-card spread

The three-card spread is the most popular spread among both beginners and advanced tarot readers. This spread typically represents the past, present, and future of a question or situation. You can position these cards anywhere, but typically you lay them in a row from left to right.

Ancestor or spirit guide spread

This tarot spread is a great way to connect with your ancestors or spirit guides during a séance.

Instructions

Prepare and open your séance according to the steps in chapter 5.

Go through your deck and remove all the court cards and either pick one intentionally to represent the spirit you want to contact (see their definitions on pages 127–32) or shuffle them and choose one at random. This will be your spirit card.

Place the spirit card in the center of your workspace.

Return the other court cards to your deck and shuffle the cards thoroughly.

When you are ready, pull one card for each of the prompts below. Be sure to look at the diagram on page 95 to learn where to place them.

0. Is the card I chose to represent you accurate? This is an optional step to begin the reading if you selected the spirit card deliberately.

1. Tell me about yourself. This card's purpose is to give you more insight into the spirit's personality so you can confirm who it is you are working with.

2. How do you make your presence known? Spirits visit us in a myriad of ways, such as in dreams. What does this spirit do?

For example, the High Priestess in this card spot may represent a spirit who whispers things or visits in dreams. The Magician could signify a spirit who flickers lights. The Ace of Pentacles could mean that this spirit leaves coins in random places.

3. What urgent message do I need to know? Spirits love to offer advice, especially to their loved ones.

4. How can I resolve the urgent message from card 3? This card represents steps to take.

5. How can I build the relationship between us? Remember that spirit communication is a two-way street: you can't just call upon ghosts whenever you need something.

6. Is there anything else you want me to know? If any Major Arcana cards come up, pull one or two more cards for this position to help clarify it.

When you are finished, thank the spirit for spending time with you and close your séance.

Paranormal investigation spread

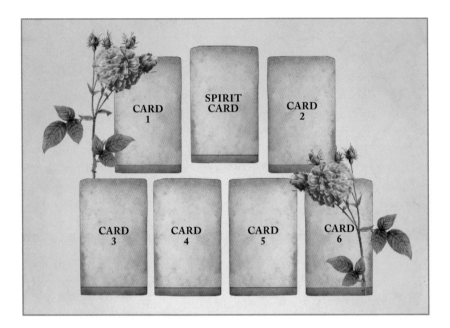

Instructions

Prepare and open your séance according to the steps in chapter 5.

Go through your deck and remove all the court cards. Shuffle these sixteen cards and choose one at random. This will be your spirit card.

Place the spirit card in the center of your workspace.

Return the other court cards to your deck and shuffle the cards thoroughly. When you are ready, pull one card for each of the prompts below.

1. Tell me about yourself. This card's purpose is to give you more insight into the spirit's personality so you can confirm who it is you are working with.

2. How did you die? If the spirit doesn't seem to know they are dead, proceed with caution or close the séance.

For example, receiving the Death card is a clear indication that the spirit is aware of their death, whereas the Eight of Swords can indicate that the spirit is confused or blind to the situation.

3. How do you make your presence known? Spirits visit us in a myriad of ways, such as in dreams. What does this spirit do?

Look for clues about how the spirit appears or communicates in the imagery of your deck. If the card has a feather on it, this could mean that the spirit leaves feathers in places they wouldn't normally be.

For example, the High Priestess in this card spot may represent a spirit who whispers things or visits in dreams. The Magician could signify a spirit who flickers lights. The Ace of Pentacles could mean that this spirit leaves coins in random places.

4. Why are you here? Sometimes spirits just have something to say and have been waiting for someone like you to ask!

5. Can I help you move on? This card can also clarify if the spirit even wants to move on. Some like to come and go or are happy where they are.

6. Is there anything else you want me to know? If any Major Arcana cards come up, pull one or two more cards for this position to help clarify it.

When you are finished, thank the spirit for spending time with you and close your séance.

RECORD KEEPING

Date:

Time:

People present:

Deck used:

Séance details (candles, heirlooms, etc.):

Spirits contacted:

Spread used or questions asked:

Court cards:

Major Arcana cards:

Minor Arcana cards:

Symbols/colors/numbers:

Notes:

CARD MEANINGS/DICTIONARY

In the following dictionary, I have included both the traditional tarot meanings and my personal spirit messages for each card. In order to understand what a spirit is attempting to communicate, it is important to have a basic understanding of each card's definition.

I encourage you to develop your own spirit messages for each card. This is known as intuitive reading. As you learned in my story about James, spirits will often use the images on the cards to convey their messages. You may be able to attach certain symbols to specific people immediately, but it may also take time and practice before patterns begin to emerge. Don't get discouraged! Be sure to use the worksheet provided to help you with this.

A QUICK NOTE ON REVERSALS: You will not find reversed meanings (when the card appears upside down) in this dictionary. I believe that with seventy-eight cards, there are enough potential combinations that any possible message or scenario imaginable can be formed without including reversals.

Understanding nuance

Because tarot is all about interpreting messages, beginners can sometimes feel overwhelmed or confused if the cards they receive don't line up 100 percent with their question. The best thing to do is take the meaning of the card and apply it directly to your specific circumstance.

Example: The Two of Cups is about a loving and caring relationship. While the default for that is a romantic relationship, it can also be about a business partnership or other interpersonal dynamics.

Understanding tense

In the following dictionary, the traditional meanings are in the present tense and sometimes the near future. This can be changed to fit the context of your reading.

Example: The Four of Wands, present tense: it's time to celebrate! The

time and energy you poured into an endeavor made it a smashing success, and you deserve a little break.

This can be changed to: The Four of Wands, past tense: it's time for the celebration to end! You took a well-deserved break after an important endeavor was successful.

MAJOR ARCANA

0: The Fool

TRADITIONAL MEANING The Fool represents the essence of the human spirit. He kicks off our journey in the tarot, making his way through the universal life milestones that all humans face. It is only natural that this card encourages taking a leap of faith and trying something new.

SPIRIT MESSAGE In a spirit reading, the Fool can represent a new soul waiting to be incarnated or be a spirit guide. If the latter, then this person has been with you all your life and ushers you in certain directions or helps you make specific decisions they find beneficial for you.

01: The Magician

TRADITIONAL MEANING The Magician is the architect of all things. He takes the raw energy of the elements and forms each one into something tangible. In a reading, the Magician encourages us to take our ideas and make something of them. Whatever you create will be successful as long as you put in the work.

SPIRIT MESSAGE This spirit is very "active" and may be able to do things like move objects and mess with electricity. You need to have firm boundaries with this person, as they could be strong enough to touch you. They aren't deliberately malicious or trying to scare you, but it can be unsettling.

02: The High Priestess

TRADITIONAL MEANING The High Priestess is all about understanding and working with your intuition and psychic gifts. She brings forward a period of spiritual growth and encourages you to follow your instincts when pondering a big decision.

SPIRIT MESSAGE The High Priestess is thought to be the keeper of the veil, and she helps guide spirits back and forth between our world and theirs. We may know intuitively when she is around, or even hear whispering in our ear.

03: The Empress

TRADITIONAL MEANING In many decks, the Empress is depicted as pregnant. This can be taken to literally represent a pregnant person, but more often than not it is a metaphor for fertility and abundance. This card encourages new ideas and bringing something great to fruition.

SPIRIT MESSAGE The Empress in a spirit reading represents a mother or grandmother figure or archetype. This person may have found a lot of joy in parenthood while alive, so it is only natural that they would continue that role in the afterlife.

04: The Emperor

TRADITIONAL MEANING The Emperor is assertive and determined in his pursuit of greatness. With this card, there is an emphasis on career or building something substantial. Success is well within your reach as long as you remain focused on your goals.

SPIRIT MESSAGE The Emperor can be the spirit of a father or grandfather figure or archetype. Their focus in life may have been on business pursuits rather than homelife. They appreciate structure, order, and ambition.

05: The Hierophant

TRADITIONAL MEANING The Hierophant represents the search for spiritual guidance and wisdom. Working with a religious leader or mentor can provide you with a new perspective and help make your hopes and dreams a reality.

SPIRIT MESSAGE This spirit enjoys providing guidance and advice. They may have been a community elder or religious leader while alive. They may be overbearing and perhaps rigid in their beliefs. They can typically be found around religious monuments and in churches.

06: The Lovers

TRADITIONAL MEANING While traditionally the Lovers card shows a romantic couple, this card can be about all sorts of harmonious and fulfilling partnerships. When this card shows up outside a love reading, it can be about making a choice between two equally appealing options. Follow your heart.

SPIRIT MESSAGE In a spirit reading, the Lovers card is generally indicative of a pair of spirits. They may have died at the same time or passed in quick succession. This card can also appear when you have lost someone you love, and they want you to know that they are watching over you, waiting for the day you are reunited.

07: The Chariot

TRADITIONAL MEANING When you need a boost of energy or the willpower to accomplish something, the Chariot is on your side. You are the commander of your life, and with a little balance, you can focus your intention and achieve greatness.

SPIRIT MESSAGE The Chariot typically signifies car wrecks or other automotive disasters. The cutting short of a life in such a traumatic way can cause confusion for spirits, and these particular ones can get attached to living people. The Chariot can also come up for military personnel, politicians, and even competitive athletes.

08: Strength

Strength can sometimes switch places with Justice and appear as number 11 in the Major Arcana.

TRADITIONAL MEANING Resilience comes from within. With the Strength card, you are being given a reminder that any obstacle you face can be defeated with determination and resolve. You possess the courage you need to overcome your fears.

SPIRIT MESSAGE When death came for this spirit, they were brave. They may have suffered through an illness such as cancer and fought the best they could. They don't want you to mourn them; they are at peace.

09: The Hermit

TRADITIONAL MEANING With the Hermit card, you know it is time to retreat into your own world and reflect on something important. This type of soul-searching can be intimidating, but confronting your traumas and preconceived notions is important for personal growth.

SPIRIT MESSAGE The Hermit represents a spirit that has haunted a location for a very long time. They are guardians of that particular space and know about all its comings and goings. This spirit could also be that of a grandparent or an older person who lived well into old age.

10: Wheel of Fortune

TRADITIONAL MEANING The Wheel of Fortune card reminds us that life is made up of cycles; when one ends, another begins. These changes are almost always positive, but remember that what goes up must also come down. Temper enthusiasm with a bit of realism.

SPIRIT MESSAGE The Wheel of Fortune in a spirit reading acknowledges the cycle of life. A death may have taken place close to where you are located. This card can also represent a residual haunting or a spirit who is repeating actions on a loop.

11: Justice

TRADITIONAL MEANING Justice is all about making decisions, but your options need to be weighed properly. Finding balance between logic and emotion can be difficult, so take a step back and take your time. Look at a situation from all angles before you choose the verdict.

SPIRIT MESSAGE This spirit may have worked in the justice system in some capacity, and perhaps even died on the job. If that doesn't apply to the situation, they may have been just a very fair and balanced person who loved to mediate or help people with their problems. This spirit may also have had trouble following the law and is hoping to make amends for mistakes they made.

12: The Hanged Man

TRADITIONAL MEANING The Hanged Man represents waiting patiently for something. He is suspended in time, but it is not against his will. While he could take action if he wanted to, he knows it is not the right time to make changes. Exercise patience.

SPIRIT MESSAGE The Hanged Man can represent a spirit of someone who died from hanging or another form of capital punishment. They like to be around the living, as they feel their life was taken from them.

13: Death

TRADITIONAL MEANING The appearance of Death in a reading signifies an ending. While painful, it is a necessary change for you to go through. You may not be able to see the silver lining right now, but you will when new life begins to bloom. If you have been putting something off, it is now time to finish it.

A spirit may be present; hold a séance!

SPIRIT MESSAGE The Death card in a spirit reading means there is a spirit willing to communicate. They understand they are dead and no confusion surrounds them. They have accepted their circumstances.

14: Temperance

TRADITIONAL MEANING Temperance is a delicate balancing act. You are an alchemist mixing up the perfect concoction, and this takes immense focus. Your current circumstances can be controlled; you just need to put mind over matter.

SPIRIT MESSAGE The Temperance card can represent a spirit who got sober from drugs or alcohol, or found religion after a difficult period in their life. This can also be a personal guardian angel for you. You may hear them whisper to you or see them in your dreams.

15: The Devil

TRADITIONAL MEANING The Devil card reminds us to think long and hard about the consequences before acting on something. You may be feeling tempted to behave badly or indulge in behaviors that could get you in trouble. Make sure you are okay with whatever the outcome will be.

SPIRIT MESSAGE The Devil in a spirit reading represents active hauntings and being afraid. Close the séance if you feel threatened in any way. This spirit may have suffered from addiction in life, or may have been in an abusive relationship. They may have also been the abuser.

16: The Tower

TRADITIONAL MEANING Your life is about to be flipped upside down when the Tower appears in your reading. Massive changes leave you feeling devastated and unsure of what to do next. Just know that this destruction was going to happen regardless of your actions. It was completely out of your control.

SPIRIT MESSAGE The death associated with this spirit was violent and unexpected. It could've been in a building collapse or some sort of workplace injury, or maybe even a shooting. This spirit likes to remind us to live our lives to the fullest, because death could come knocking at any time.

17: The Star

TRADITIONAL MEANING The Star brings feelings of hope and peace after chaos. Positivity and blessings are heading toward you, so make a wish and it just may be granted!

SPIRIT MESSAGE The Star represents someone who periodically visits you to make sure you are on the right track. When things seem to be at their darkest, they encourage you to keep going. In life, this spirit may have been a champion for the disenfranchised, or spent their time trying to make the world a better place.

18: The Moon

TRADITIONAL MEANING Uncertainty, fears, and disillusionment are the domain of the Moon card. This could be a confusing period of time for you. There isn't enough information available to you to make a decision about something, so you need to turn to your intuition.

SPIRIT MESSAGE The Moon signifies a spirit who is hiding in the shadows, and they aren't ready to reveal themselves. This could be a child who is shy, or someone who doesn't yet realize they are dead. They could be feeling disoriented and pass this feeling on to you.

19: The Sun

TRADITIONAL MEANING Joy, abundance, and good times are the energy of the Sun card. This card fills you with self-confidence, and you will be rewarded for your natural gifts and talents. Go on and bask in the spotlight; you earned it.

SPIRIT MESSAGE The Sun signifies that you are in the presence of a very happy spirit. In life, they would be described as being cheerful, and their positive mindset was infectious to those around them. They always made the best of their circumstances and continue that practice in the spirit world.

20: Judgment

TRADITIONAL MEANING The Judgment card says to take some time to reevaluate your priorities and what you want out of life. If something isn't working, let it go and don't look back. The time for change and personal reinvention is now. Become your authentic self.

SPIRIT MESSAGE Judgment in a spirit reading can symbolize a very religious individual or someone who feels they need to repent. They may not be able to move on until they feel they are forgiven for past sins. This spirit may also make you feel physically ill.

21: The World

TRADITIONAL MEANING The World in a reading asks you to look back over your life (or recent past) with admiration. While you may have faced setbacks and obstacles, you have also achieved many great things. Use this time for enjoyment and relaxation, as a new cycle is about to begin.

SPIRIT MESSAGE This spirit had a life that many would envy. They may have been wealthy, or known abundance in some way. They don't have any "unfinished business" and don't see the point in haunting the living, though they do like to periodically check in.

MINOR ARCANA

Wands

The suit of Wands is ruled by the element of fire. They deal with the parts of life that are creative, passionate, and spiritual.

They are the liveliest of the Minor Arcana, and cover a broad range of everyday scenarios. Think joyous celebrations, accomplishing goals, hot tempers, and lovers' quarrels.

I like to relate the Wands to the Major Arcana. Where the Majors show us the grandest parts of the human experience, the Wands scale down those energies to fit into everyday life. This should not be confused with being mundane, because their fiery core is anything but.

The Wands also tend to show us where movement, action, and change are required in our lives. They are sudden flashes of inspiration that can be channeled into both productivity and enjoyment.

When communicating with a spirit, the Wands talk to us about either a person or a situation that was energetic, dynamic, and dominant.

These are generally the people who spoke before thinking, made natural leaders, and had more projects on the go than they had time for.

Ace of Wands

TRADITIONAL MEANING The ace represents the initial spark of an idea or creative pursuit. Harness inspiration and let it lead you to greatness. Following your instincts is the best course of action, but stay on the path: it can be easy to get distracted right now.

SPIRIT MESSAGE This spirit was an inventive and passionate person who always seemed to make something out of nothing. They may have smoked cigarettes or a pipe, and perhaps died due to the negative health effects. They also took plenty of risks, sometimes to the detriment of others or themselves. The Ace of Wands also represents a playful or mischievous spirit who likes to play games with the occupants of a home.

Two of Wands

TRADITIONAL MEANING Careful planning is in order for success in the future. The things you want to do can be done, but you must not skip vital steps in your rush to the end. You would be wise to think before acting.

SPIRIT MESSAGE A spirit who never got the chance to realize their dreams. Passions were stifled due to responsibility or oppressive standards of their time. They were forced to make a choice between two desires.

Three of Wands

TRADITIONAL MEANING This card is one of the wish fulfillment cards in the deck. Whatever work you put into your ideas now will reap benefits three times as great. Though it is imperative to exercise a bit of patience when you are waiting for your reward, trust in the knowledge that it will find you.

SPIRIT MESSAGE A spirit who is longing for a lost love. They may have a strong connection to large bodies of water. They were an avid traveler in their day. The Three of Wands could mean they are waiting for someone to return, or the inability to move on. Perhaps they are still holding on to hope that the outcome will be different.

Four of Wands

TRADITIONAL MEANING It is time to celebrate! The time and energy you poured into an endeavor made it a smashing success, and you deserve a little break. This card also says there is no shortage of people willing to honor you, so go on and throw that party.

SPIRIT MESSAGE We're dealing with the spirit of a family member or close friend. They were considered the life of the party. They may have been a fantastic storyteller, always keeping people on the edge of their seats. This spirit likes to attend all the important family events.

Five of Wands

TRADITIONAL MEANING Conflict, chaos, and rivalry reign. You have been pushed into battle, and only the best of the best will come out on top. Now is the time to call on your many skills and talents to make sure you are that person. You would do well not to be cocky, though, as your opponent may have some tricks up their sleeve.

SPIRIT MESSAGE A spirit who fought in a war, or perhaps even died in one. Anger seemed to surround this person in life, despite their attempts to move away from it. They seem to dwell on past arguments and mistakes they once made.

Six of Wands

TRADITIONAL MEANING Victory is yours, and your hard work will not go unnoticed by higher-ups. If this accomplishment is work-related, you could be offered a promotion; otherwise, think of this moment as spiritually "leveling up." But remember: When you are at the top, there is always someone looking to knock you back down.

SPIRIT MESSAGE This spirit spent a lot of time trying to improve themselves and their circumstances. They may have taken on the role of the champion or savior to help the disenfranchised. A protective energy accompanies them, and they hope to offer you sound advice.

Seven of Wands

TRADITIONAL MEANING The best defense is a good offense—cliché, but true. You may be feeling attacked from all angles right now. There is a feeling of pressure and urgency that comes with this situation, but hold your ground and don't let anyone push you around.

SPIRIT MESSAGE Fighting was a major theme of this spirit's life: fighting with loved ones, fighting to earn money, fighting to keep their possessions, fighting to be accepted. They may have been forced to conform to heteronormative standards or defend their love for someone.

Eight of Wands

TRADITIONAL MEANING Sudden action and rapid movement is the energy of this card. You aren't choosing to move forward so much as you are being pushed. The universe has a plan and you'd better get on board or you may be left behind. Ultimately this card is a positive omen, and anything you attempt to do will be successful.

SPIRIT MESSAGE This spirit was (or maybe still is) constantly on the move. They always had a full social calendar but made sure they gave the person they were with their undivided attention. Living life to the fullest was a priority, and they may be disappointed if their life was suddenly cut short.

Nine of Wands

TRADITIONAL MEANING The Nine of Wands arrives when you feel like you cannot take one more step toward the finish line, but you have no choice but to press on. You are battered and broken, but giving up is not part of your vocabulary.

SPIRIT MESSAGE A lot of strife and conflict surrounded this spirit. They may have suffered some sort of abuse in their life, or may have actually themselves been the abuser. Soldiers and people who died in combat can also feel a kinship with the Nine of Wands.

Ten of Wands

TRADITIONAL MEANING Whatever project you took on is beginning to feel a lot like a burden. The Ten of Wands poses the question, do I continue carrying this bundle around because it's what I am used to, or do I drop these sticks and pick up something else? Too much responsibility is unhealthy for anybody, so it may be time to take a break.

SPIRIT MESSAGE Deadlines, children, errands, and stress. This spirit may have been an overworked and underappreciated housewife, or even an employee who did too much for their boss. They often felt unsupported by their partner, or were perhaps even abandoned by them and left to shoulder all major responsibilities alone.

Pentacles

The suit of Pentacles (also called coins) is ruled by the element of earth. They deal with matters of the material plane, like money, nature, and the physical body.

Situations relating to stability, security, health, and career are the domain of the Pentacles. They bring a fresh dose of balance and realism to the tarot.

The Pentacles are tangible. They are the thing you can reach out and grab. Manifestation is also a big part of this suit, whether it is physical or spiritual.

Because this suit is connected to the earth, there is also a nurturing quality to it. These cards show you where there is room to grow and also what needs to be healed.

When communicating with a spirit, the Pentacles talk about a person who was determined, self-assured, and hardworking. Their career and hobbies may have been an enormous part of their life. They were the type of person who was always trying to better themselves and their circumstances.

Ace of Pentacles

TRADITIONAL MEANING The Ace of Pentacles represents "all that could be." It is raw, earthly energy that is just waiting to be shaped and formed into something of substance. In some cases, this card represents actual money, and therefore some may be on its way to you. With the right approach, you can grow this wind-fall into something even more substantial.

SPIRIT MESSAGE This card can mean a spirit is concerned about their life's work, or what is happening with the money they left behind for their family. Disputes over wills trouble them, and they may leave signs around hoping to clarify what their intentions were at death. You may also feel their presence when they are around or find coins in unexpected places.

Two of Pentacles

TRADITIONAL MEANING When the Two of Pentacles appears, it often feels as though all you're doing lately is juggling two equally important things in your life. This can be a delicate balancing act between your job and your social life, or your health and your family, but you can't keep this up forever. While both things have immense value to you, you may need to pick one to be your sole focus in the short term so you are no longer dividing your attention.

SPIRIT MESSAGE In life, this spirit may have felt like they never had the time for all the things they valued. Or they were busy doing so many things they rarely took a break to do what they enjoyed. The Two of Pentacles can also reference someone who comes and goes between worlds frequently.

Three of Pentacles

TRADITIONAL MEANING The time is right to collaborate with others on a project. If you are used to taking the lead or working alone, you may find this difficult. Remember that you can actually learn a lot from other people, and may even uncover ways to improve your own skill set. The Three of Pentacles is also about hard work and study, so now is a great time to dedicate yourself to your goals.

SPIRIT MESSAGE The Three of Pentacles represents a spirit who embodies the idea of the "team player." They enjoy working with others and communicating with the living. They were also dedicated to their many hobbies and interests, often locking themselves away for periods of time to get things done. This spirit may also check in or watch over you in a protective manner.

Four of Pentacles

TRADITIONAL MEANING Holding on too tightly to resources is just as dangerous as being too loose with them. When it comes to things like wealth and abundance, there needs to be a bit of breathing room in order for them to grow. Are you being frugal or are you being greedy?

SPIRIT MESSAGE When the Four of Pentacles shows up, you can be certain you are dealing with a spirit who is stubborn and strong-willed. They may also feel energetically tied to a particular place, object, or even person. In life they would be described as frugal, perhaps even cheap, and they didn't appreciate being parted from their resources.

Five of Pentacles

TRADITIONAL MEANING Poverty and health issues are the themes of the Five of Pentacles. Financial struggles often bring shame, which naturally leads to a reluctance to ask for help. Sometimes, when facing adversity, you need to swallow your pride and do what is best for yourself and your family. If you have been facing significant health problems, it may feel like there is no end in sight, but remember that tomorrow is a new day.

SPIRIT MESSAGE A lot of sadness is connected with the Five of Pentacles. It can mean that the spirit suffered a lot in their life. Financial problems, lack of food, chronic health conditions, or mental health struggles may have been an ever-constant presence.

Six of Pentacles

TRADITIONAL MEANING With the Six of Pentacles, you are being offered relief from troubling situations. Someone is coming to your rescue, and they will help you get back on your feet. If you have been searching for answers about a specific situation, rest assured, the answer is on its way. Unexpected resources also have a tendency to turn up now, and this has a positive impact.

SPIRIT MESSAGE In life, this spirit was always there to lend a helping hand. They may have been a community leader or respected mentor. They may still leave gifts for the living in the form of coins. This is a great person to call on for advice when you are stuck.

Seven of Pentacles

TRADITIONAL MEANING Seeds you previously planted are busy underground growing roots. The Seven of Pentacles is a good reminder that just because you aren't seeing the fruits of your labor yet, it doesn't mean nothing is happening. Exercising some patience is important right now. Little changes over time are what bring the biggest results in the end.

SPIRIT MESSAGE This spirit would have been described as the strong, silent type, and they probably still embody those qualities. This isn't the type of ghost to rattle doorknobs or put on a show; they prefer subtle and more thoughtful gestures to make their presence known. They could get attached to others, and may work as a "welcome committee" for recently deceased people.

Eight of Pentacles

TRADITIONAL MEANING Now is when you need to step up and put in a lot of hard work. If you have big dreams, turning them into reality is possible, but you need to remain dedicated. If you have been wanting to learn a new skill, you are being offered an abundance of energy not only to become good at it but to master it.

SPIRIT MESSAGE Craftspeople, entrepreneurs, and inventors are often represented with the Eight of Pentacles. These spirits left a meaningful impact on the world, and they are still quite proud of that. This card can also be a reference to a parent who is looking down on their children with immense pride.

Nine of Pentacles

TRADITIONAL MEANING Positivity, abundance, and good times all around! The Nine of Pentacles is one of the wish fulfillment cards in the deck and a great omen to receive. Take a look around you and see everything you have accomplished. You have more than enough and can enjoy a little excess now. Taking pride in yourself tells the universe you are open to receiving even more.

SPIRIT MESSAGE The Nine of Pentacles in a spirit reading talks about a glamorous person who lived a lavish lifestyle. They loved to buy the finer things, throw big parties, and celebrate life. Sometimes, though, these spirits indulged a little too much and made a mess of their personal relationships. These spirits may be overly attached to heirlooms and jewelry.

Ten of Pentacles

TRADITIONAL MEANING With the Ten of Pentacles, you have reached the end of a journey on a positive note. Everything you have built and worked for is paid off. You avoided shortcuts and shady dealings, and built a solid foundation made of integrity. Your health should be good right now too, but continue to make it a priority. How can you help others with the abundance you have acquired? Doing good deeds builds character.

SPIRIT MESSAGE Generational wealth, inheritance, and familial connection are all part of the Ten of Pentacles. If you recently received an inheritance, just know that this spirit is happy to provide a brighter future for you. If they weren't able to leave anything physical, they sometimes want to remind you of the emotional and spiritual qualities they instilled in you. These spirits tend to be triggered by the sale of homes or assets, so be mindful and compassionate.

Swords

The suit of Swords is ruled by the element of air. These cards deal with the parts of life that are intellectual, powerful, and complicated.

They are considered to be the most difficult of the Minor Arcana, likely due to their rulership of the mind and the conflicting nature of the different thoughts we possess at any given time.

Their energy can be logical and brilliant one moment and cutting and cold the next. Communication, planning, resolution, and fear are generally represented by this suit.

The Swords show us things we haven't wanted to face but must in order to heal and grow. Often painful, these situations tend to change who we are—for better or for worse.

When communicating with spirits, we should know that this suit represents people who hid their emotions often, and who come across as logical but also critical.

They may have worked in the field of science, academia, or law, or even been writers.

Situations relating to the Swords were likely stressful and deeply painful. Murder, accidents, or other sudden deaths can also be reflected in this suit, so it is imperative to approach these cards with compassion and patience.

Ace of Swords

TRADITIONAL MEANING The Ace of Swords embodies raw intellectual energy. It is pulsing and magnetic, ready to be channeled into a new plan or idea. Think of this card as the breakthrough you've been waiting for. But like all swords, it has a double edge, so take extra precaution.

SPIRIT MESSAGE This card represents a spirit who is willing and ready to communicate. They may have been described as a "chatty Cathy" type or unafraid to speak their mind. The Ace of Swords can also represent surgery, which may have been a recurring theme throughout their life or even a cause of death.

Two of Swords

TRADITIONAL MEANING When you are faced with a tough decision, the Two of Swords tends to appear. You are standing at a crossroads and need time to balance both options before landing on which path to take. This decision should be made rationally, so take your time with it.

SPIRIT MESSAGE This spirit is not ready to accept the circumstances of their death. They often feel caught between worlds, and this may have been the case in their life as well. They were someone who struggled to make substantial choices, or worried about making the wrong one so much that they never actually accomplished anything.

Three of Swords

TRADITIONAL MEANING Heartbreak and disappointment are the predominant energies of the Three of Swords. These feelings are often due to some sort of betrayal or rejection by another person. While right now you are going through a depressing period of time, just know it won't last forever.

SPIRIT MESSAGE The Three of Swords represents a great pain that took place during a spirit's life. They may still be suffering the effects of this and aren't sure how to move on. They may have also died suddenly, leaving a lot of unanswered questions and pain for their loved ones.

Four of Swords

TRADITIONAL MEANING After a period of stress or other challenges, it is best to take a time-out. The Four of Swords is a welcome reminder that it is okay to do nothing. You have been running on empty and deserve a break. This card can also mean you need to start making your mental health a priority.

SPIRIT MESSAGE This spirit may have been sick for a while before death. They were likely also regarded as the strong, silent type, so seeing them suffer would've been difficult on their family. They may also be happy to finally get a break from their pain, but not quite ready to move on, so they are watching the world go by from the sidelines.

Five of Swords

TRADITIONAL MEANING The Five of Swords brings conflict, strife, and intellectual warfare. Being in the midst of an argument can lead you to say things you don't actually mean. It may feel good in the moment, but you will be celebrating your cruel victory all alone.

SPIRIT MESSAGE The energy surrounding this card is very heavy. This spirit may have suffered through a lot of emotional abuse, with their homelife full of conflict. Of course, they could also be the one who inflicted pain on others, and they may have a lot of regrets. Sometimes the Five of Swords shows a feeling of inner turmoil. Finding peace is difficult for this spirit because they can't ask for forgiveness on the other side.

Six of Swords

TRADITIONAL MEANING You've done everything you can in a situation, and it is time to move on to something else. Think of the Six of Swords as your ticket to freedom: freedom from pain, freedom from suffering, and, most importantly, freedom to begin again. We all have situations we are afraid to let go of, but if we don't, we may miss out on new things coming.

SPIRIT MESSAGE This is a spirit who is just passing through. This card shows up shortly after death and indicates a short stay. They have accepted their circumstance and are excited to see what comes next. Allow them to move on and don't let their passing control your life.

Seven of Swords

TRADITIONAL MEANING Betrayal and deception are two things none of us want to deal with, but unfortunately, they are part of life. Someone may have lied to you or tricked you in some way, and now you're left to clean up the mess. It could also be that you are trying to get away with deceiving someone else. You may be successful, but you have to ask yourself: at what cost?

SPIRIT MESSAGE This spirit is a bit of a trickster. You may notice things missing from their usual place, only to reappear the next day. The Seven of Swords can also be about someone who lied a lot in their lifetime. They may be confused now about which stories were real and which were their own elaborate inventions. Cause of death could be a mystery. Proceed with caution.

Eight of Swords

TRADITIONAL MEANING If you are feeling trapped by your circumstances, it may not be comforting to know that they are of your own making. The Eight of Swords didn't put you in confinement: you did. Luckily, this jail is temporary, and you can remove your shackles and bonds when you're ready.

SPIRIT MESSAGE This card could be about physically being in a real jail, not just an internal or metaphorical one. If the spirit in question spent time in prison, they may be fixated on making amends. This card also represents a spirit who feels trapped and is refusing to accept that they are dead.

Nine of Swords

TRADITIONAL MEANING The Nine of Swords is one of the most stressful cards to get in a reading. It represents a period of sleepless nights and feeling filled with anxiety. No matter what you do, negative and self-limiting beliefs flood your consciousness. If you aren't careful, these fears may become reality in the form of a self-fulfilling prophecy.

SPIRIT MESSAGE A spirit (or spirits) may be visiting you at night or even appear in your dreams. Their presence may be unnerving, but they don't mean to frighten you. This card can also be about someone who suffered from anxiety or was a bit of a worrywart. They may have also caused stress to others or been a hypochondriac.

Ten of Swords

TRADITIONAL MEANING With the Ten of Swords, you have reached a painful ending or conclusion to something. This card brings with it grief and despair, and you may wonder if you'll ever feel happy again. But rest assured, you will. On the bright side—though it may be hard to see—remember that with every death, a new life begins.

SPIRIT MESSAGE This spirit was stabbed in the back, either literally or metaphorically. They know they should accept their circumstances but aren't quite ready to forgive those who wronged them. While alive, they may have also been the type to "drink poison and expect their enemy to die," and they aren't sure what to do now that they are the ones who are actually dead.

Cups

The suit of Cups is ruled by the element of water. These cards deal with the parts of life that are emotional, intimate, and nostalgic.

Relationships, family life, dreams, and memories are ruled by the Cups. They are intuitive and idealistic, encouraging us to look inside ourselves for guidance.

The Cups are an "all or nothing" type of energy. They range from absolute bliss to utter despair. Balancing this vast range of emotions takes work.

In terms of spirit communication, this suit tends to describe people who were compassionate, emotional, and empathetic. These spirits may have also been overly sensitive at times, or were prone to selfish behavior.

The Cups come with a warning about spirits who had substance abuse issues and continuous struggles with depression.

Ace of Cups

TRADITIONAL MEANING The Ace of Cups contains raw emotional energy. While this is generally a positive omen, you need to channel it into something productive. If you sit with it for too long, it can grow stale and even morph into resentment. The Ace of Cups also represents a pregnancy or a budding new romance.

SPIRIT MESSAGE The Ace of Cups is an acknowledgment from a spirit about a new job, a new baby, or other big changes their family members are experiencing. While they were alive, they showed their affection with food and drink and expensive gifts.

Two of Cups

TRADITIONAL MEANING A new, exciting, and fulfilling relationship is on the horizon. There is a lot of mutual attraction and respect between you. The Two of Cups makes this partnership quite strong, and together you feel as though you can take on the world. But remember that good things still require patience and hard work.

SPIRIT MESSAGE This card signals a spirit who is waiting for their partner or loved one before they move on. They may have faced prejudice or been kept apart due to cultural differences, which led to obstacles in their relationship. This spirit is very active in love readings and feels a duty to offer advice.

Three of Cups

TRADITIONAL MEANING Good friends and good times are the embodiment of the Three of Cups. Everything is smooth sailing, and you're looking forward to spending time with the people you love most.

SPIRIT MESSAGE This card typically represents a group of spirits who are great friends to both you and one another. They love to offer advice and are great allies to have when inquiring about personal matters, especially anything regarding relationships.

Four of Cups

TRADITIONAL MEANING The Four of Cups represents someone being in a state of melancholy. You may feel bored and disinterested in things you once loved but are too fixated on feeling bad to try anything new. Really take some time to look inward and figure out what it is you want to do in life. The answer may surprise you.

SPIRIT MESSAGE The Four of Cups can appear when dealing with spirits who struggled with substance abuse or depression. They may have also been self-absorbed or had a disregard for people's boundaries due to childhood trauma.

Five of Cups

TRADITIONAL MEANING The Five of Cups brings major emotional setbacks, usually in the form of a loss. This hurts deeply and will take time to heal. Even though it feels like this mindset will last forever, it won't. Focus on moving forward.

SPIRIT MESSAGE This spirit is surrounded by a lot of sadness and disappointment. Because they faced many setbacks in life, they either can't move on or refuse to move on. This card can also represent a residual spirit whose energy replays on a loop.

Six of Cups

TRADITIONAL MEANING The Six of Cups is all about the nostalgia of youth. Fond memories of first loves can bring a lot of comfort, but make sure you aren't living in the past; try to find things in your present that trigger those same feelings.

SPIRIT MESSAGE The Six of Cups can relate to the spirit of a child or someone who died too young. This could also be someone you were very close to, like a sibling, cousin, or old friend. They like to take on the role of a spirit guide and encourage you to be more playful.

Seven of Cups

TRADITIONAL MEANING Being spoiled for choice isn't always a good thing. The Seven of Cups brings a lot of options, both positive and negative, and it is your job to figure out which is best for you. You run the risk of having your "head stuck in the clouds" if you wait too long to make a decision.

SPIRIT MESSAGE This spirit could be described as a dreamer. They were always on to the next big thing. They could never seem to hold on to their money and may have been a shopaholic, or they may have struggled with gambling or showed their love with material things. They tend to come and go as they please and are a bit flaky.

Eight of Cups

TRADITIONAL MEANING This is a card about leaving something behind—not necessarily because you want to, but because you have to. The Eight of Cups is a very sad card, but try and remember that tomorrow is a new day.

SPIRIT MESSAGE A spirit who communicates using the Eight of Cups tends to leave for extended periods of time. You may think they have gone for good, only to have them turn back up unexpectedly. They probably faced significant setbacks in their life or were divorced multiple times. Unfortunately, the Eight of Cups can also represent a spirit who ended their life. *If you or someone you know is thinking about suicide, please reach out for support.*

Nine of Cups

TRADITIONAL MEANING As one of the wish fulfillment cards in the tarot, the Nine of Cups urges you to go ahead and dream big. You are full of self-confidence and happiness, and any support you need will be there.

SPIRIT MESSAGE The Nine of Cups symbolizes a spirit who is happy and enjoying their time on the other side. They likely lived into old age, and didn't have much in the way of "unfinished business." This spirit may be very active, move things around your home, or even visit you in your dreams.

Ten of Cups

TRADITIONAL MEANING You have everything you could want and more. The Ten of Cups speaks of harmony, positivity, and a healthy and secure homelife. You may be more focused on romance than usual, and this is a good thing. Love is definitely heading your way.

SPIRIT MESSAGE This card is often connected to a protective, guardian-type spirit. You may see them out of the corner of your eye or catch a glimpse of them in your mirror. They may be the patriarch of your family, or someone you looked up to, such as an older sibling.

The court cards

Each suit of the Minor Arcana contains four additional cards known as the court cards. These named figures represent either ourselves or people in our lives. Sometimes these cards can be about situations, but for the purpose of this book and spirit communication, the court cards will always be people.

I highly recommend removing all the court cards from the deck temporarily when doing a spirit reading. These sixteen cards will be used to identify who you are speaking to. You can shuffle and draw one at random, or if you have someone specific in mind, you can go through and pick a card that represents them best. Once you've done that, you can return the remaining cards to the deck.

Page of Wands

Age or maturity level: Child or teen
Zodiac: Aries, Leo, or Sagittarius
Personality traits: Caring, curious, noisy, imaginative, naive

The Page of Wands is a creative and highly imaginative individual. They were never afraid to take risks in life, which made them courageous, but they often suffered consequences for these actions. They may have died young, or had a "young at heart" approach to life.

Knight of Wands

Age or maturity level: Young adult
Zodiac: Sagittarius
Personality traits: Expressive, fickle, outspoken, energetic, exhibitionist

Confident, enthusiastic, and full of charm best describes the Knight of Wands personality. This individual needed a lot of freedom in their life, and may have

had trouble committing to relationships or jobs. While you could count on them for a good time, they weren't really around when the going got tough.

Queen of Wands

Age or maturity level: Middle-aged adult
Zodiac: Aries
Personality traits: Artistic, creative, jealous, brash, biting

The Queen of Wands embodies the entrepreneurial spirit. They are passionate, boisterous, and independent. While alive, they would've been the person at the center of their social group, always making new friends. You had to be careful not to cross them, however, as their temper was legendary.

King of Wands

Age or maturity level: Older adult
Zodiac: Leo
Personality traits: Proud, enthusiastic, egotistical, loyal, warmhearted

Like the queen of this suit, the King of Wands is a natural leader. They could captivate an audience without breaking a sweat. Fiercely loyal and protective, you could always turn to them for advice, but since they were so direct, sometimes they told you what you didn't want to hear.

Page of Pentacles

Age or maturity level: Child or teen
Zodiac: Taurus, Virgo, or Capricorn
Personality traits: Focused, reliable, eager, bossy, know-it-all

Responsible and focused, the Page of Pentacles is one of those "old soul" individuals who probably acted much like an adult even in childhood. They thrived in environments where their thoughts were valued and likely sought out multiple degrees or certificates. The pressure to be the best may have made them a bit bossy or a bit of a know-it-all.

Knight of Pentacles

Age or maturity level: Young adult
Zodiac: Virgo
Personality traits: Hardworking, deliberate, thoughtful, patient, prejudiced

Unlike the other knights, the Knight of Pentacles is patient and deliberate in their actions. In life they were described as being frugal, or perhaps even cheap, but really, they just understood the value of things. Because they took their time with everything, they weren't much of a self-starter.

Queen of Pentacles

Age or maturity level: Middle-aged adult
Zodiac: Capricorn
Personality traits: Nurturing, maternal, generous, critical

The Queen of Pentacles is a nurturing and reliable partner. This person had many natural gifts and hobbies throughout their life. They showed their love with acts of service or by giving gifts—which were always handmade. Because they always looked out for others, they may have neglected their own needs or feelings.

King of Pentacles

Age or maturity level: Older adult
Zodiac: Taurus
Personality traits: Stable, determined, hardworking, pretentious

The King of Pentacles could be described as determined, stable, and proficient. If they weren't monetarily rich while alive, they were definitely rich in companionship and accomplishments. Because they were naturally ambitious, they may have looked down on others for not working as hard as they did.

Page of Swords

Age or maturity level: Child or teen
Zodiac: Gemini, Libra, or Aquarius
Personality traits: Shy, inquisitive, introverted, adaptable, critical

This individual could be described as having an insatiable appetite for learning. Witty, smart, and adaptable, the Page of Swords was the type of person who was always asking questions, sometimes to the annoyance of those around them. They had a young energy, even if they lived well into old age, likely due to their natural curiosity about the world around them.

Knight of Swords

Age or maturity level: Young adult
Zodiac: Gemini
Personality traits: Stimulating, quick-witted, curious, moody, intrusive

The Knight of Swords is both talkative and opinionated. They strive to be the best of the best and in life were always doing what they could to better themselves and their circumstances. Because they were also impatient, they could be harsh or overly critical toward their loved ones at times.

Queen of Swords

Age or maturity level: Middle-aged adult
Zodiac: Libra
Personality traits: Ambitious, analytical, harsh, independent, biased

The Queen of Swords is an introverted individual. They prefer their own company in death just as they did in life. Because they are so perceptive, they may have had trouble opening up to people. But when they did finally let someone in, that person would gain a loyal friend and confidant.

King of Swords

Age or maturity level: Older adult
Zodiac: Aquarius
Personality traits: Logical, savvy, trustworthy, authoritative, inflexible

Both logical and fair, the King of Swords is someone you want on your side in a dispute or conflict. They worked hard throughout their life and made good providers, but this didn't leave much time for social engagement or fun, and their family may have found them overly harsh or critical.

Page of Cups

Age or maturity level: Child or teen
Zodiac: Cancer, Scorpio, or Pisces
Personality traits: Sensitive, sweet, timid, passive-aggressive

Filled to the brim with sweetness, the Page of Cups is the type of person everyone wants in their life. Because they were so sensitive, they sometimes got caught up in other people's drama. They may have put on a brave face, but inside they were timid and insecure.

Knight of Cups

Age or maturity level: Young adult
Zodiac: Pisces
Personality traits: Erratic, friendly, jovial, clingy, tactless

The Knight of Cups is a friendly and gregarious personality type. In life, they pursued many different passions and dreams, and there was no limit to their emotional depth. Unfortunately, nothing and nobody could truly live up to this knight's ideals and fantasies, so they may have faced repeated disappointments.

Queen of Cups

Age or maturity level: Middle-aged adult
Zodiac: Cancer
Personality traits: Intuitive, compassionate, humble, reactive, superficial

Warmth and compassion are two of the qualities this queen embodies. They are intuitive and may have been considered to be psychic or even a little "witchy" while alive. Because they were naturally empathetic, they could sometimes be overly reactionary or even volatile, which may have put a strain on their relationships.

King of Cups

Age or maturity level: Older adult
Zodiac: Scorpio
Personality traits: Kind, affectionate, responsible, arrogant, vengeful

The King of Cups is emotionally intelligent and kind. They were the type of person who lit up a room just by being in it. While in their day-to-day life they tended to keep their emotions in check, if angered or hurt, they could be awfully vengeful and petty.

7

Automatic Writing

WHAT IS AUTOMATIC WRITING?

Have you ever doodled while talking on the phone? Most people would answer yes. When we do that, we are reacting unconsciously, unaware of what our hand is doing. Our conscious mind is occupied with the conversation we are having.

The process of psychography, a.k.a. automatic writing, works in a similar way.

During an automatic writing session, ideas and thoughts are believed to be telepathically communicated from a spirit through the writer onto the paper. This naturally makes it an interesting form of channeling.

It can be assumed that automatic writing has been around for as long as humans have been recording language, though there is no definitive origin story to be found. Automatic writing reached its peak in the nineteenth century during the height of spiritualism, and it is also still a popular choice for mediums today.

Some people don't write during these sessions, but instead draw, sketch, or paint.

And while this practice comes naturally for some people, it is typically thought to be one of the more difficult methods of divination. Part of the reason for this is internal skepticism. It can be hard at first to determine whether you're actually channeling from a spirit or if the words are coming from a higher version of yourself.

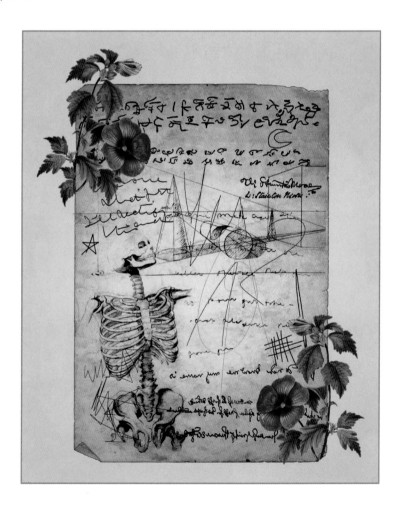

Because of this, many people give up on automatic writing before they have given it a fair chance.

I recommend working on automatic writing for a minimum of three months before deciding it isn't for you. Try different techniques!

PARANORMAL STORY AND HISTORY

Did automatic writing help uncover some of the lost ruins of Glastonbury Abbey in the early 1900s? The man credited with their discovery certainly thought so!

Frederick Bligh Bond was a true renaissance man. An archaeologist, architect, illustrator, and, later, psychical researcher, he had no shortage of skills, but the one he would become famous for is automatic writing.

In 1908, the Church of England appointed Bond director in charge of the search and excavations of Glastonbury Abbey, in Somerset, England. The abbey was originally built in the eighth century and served as a monastery.

With political and religious alliances shifting all the time, and with the Normans invading England a few centuries later, many monks were killed at the abbey for their resistance to new leadership.

In the late 1100s, many of the original buildings were destroyed in a fire, including the original church itself. However, rebuilding commenced, beginning with a new house of worship.

Some years later, the monks living at the abbey announced that they had discovered the bones of the legendary King Arthur and Queen Guinevere. Many people today believe this was an elaborate stunt to secure more funding from the then current king.

From the fourteenth to sixteenth centuries, Glastonbury Abbey was at its peak of wealth and influence. However, in 1534 King Henry VIII began his quest to separate England from Catholicism, which led to the dissolution of the monasteries. Glastonbury saw its own end in 1539, with the execution of the abbot Richard Whiting.

From here, the abbey and its buildings were gifted to the then Duke of Somerset, who didn't seem to want to be bothered with them.

Many of the stones were removed and used to construct new buildings and roads in the town, and little by little, the once powerful abbey became a lifeless shell.

That is, until Bond came into the picture.

Bond rediscovered the outlines, dimensions, and stones for many of the buildings that had once stood on the site, long hidden under centuries of dirt and grass.

This was a career-defining achievement for an archaeologist. In 1918 Bond felt ready to reveal the secret of his knowledge and success at the abbey, and he published a book called *The Gate of Remembrance*.

In it, Bond claimed that—with the help of his friend the retired captain and proclaimed psychic medium John Allan Bartlett—he had been in contact with a deceased monk who had provided them with the locations of where to dig. These communications took place during automatic writing sessions involving the two living men.

When the Church of England, which at the time vehemently opposed spiritualism, discovered the book in 1921, Bond was relieved of his duties at Glastonbury. The church was so angry that it went as far as stripping him of his ceremonial key.

Bond, who was steadfast in his convictions, would go on to become the editor of the magazine *Quarterly Transactions of the British College of Psychic Science*, and also became a member of the famous organizations the Society for Psychical Research and the Ghost Club. The latter was the oldest official paranormal organization in the world.

Whether you believe that Bond found the ruins via automatic writing or not, the fact remains that he believed it, and until he turned up at Glastonbury, the locations of those sites remained hidden.

Bond could have kept the reason behind his success a secret in order to protect his reputation. Perhaps he felt indebted to the old monk who had been waiting there all those years for just the right person to come along.

The role of automatic writing in history isn't reserved to divination. Through automatic writing, women found the means to flex their creative muscles.

UTENSILS FOR THE PURPOSE OF

AUTOMATIC WRITING

Soft Pastel Crayons.

Premium Quality ..**6**/- per dozen.

Common Quality ..**4**/- per dozen.

Lead Pencils, in Boxes.

Premium Quality ..**6**/- per dozen.

Common Quality ..**4**/- per dozen.

Cedar Pencils.

2/- per dozen.

The wives of famous authors—such as William Butler Yeats—delighted the general public with their writings, something they would have never had the opportunity to do had they not taken up mediumship.

Jean Leckie, the second wife of Sir Arthur Conan Doyle, was inspired by her husband's passion for spiritualism, and while in automatic writing sessions, she produced hundreds of pages of text, the words apparently given to her by a companion spirit of the couple.

Automatic writing not only gave women a creative voice; it also helped shape copyright law.

In London in 1927, a well-known medium named Geraldine Dorothy Cummins brought forth a lawsuit against—of all people—Frederick Bligh Bond.

Once upon a time, Cummins and Bond had shared a love for Glastonbury Abbey and the automatic writing Bond had produced there. The pair decided it would be in their best interest to participate in a séance together along with Cummins's assistant, Edith Beatrice Gibbes. It was a great experience for all, so the trio made it a regular thing.

On one occasion, Cummins produced a uniquely specific piece of work that Bond recognized as a form of sixteenth-century English.

Bond took it upon himself to translate the words into a more legible and modern tongue. When finished, he decided to have a sample published in one of the magazines he was involved with.

The piece was a hit with the paranormal community, and Bond attempted to convince the women to split ownership of the text three ways, so he could have free rein to publish all of it as he saw fit.

Cummins felt pressured and decided she did not want to split the copyright and asked for her work back.

When Bond refused, the women were forced to file a lawsuit.

During the hearing, Bond claimed that the work actually belonged to the spirit, known to them as Cleophas, and therefore Cummins had no right to take back ownership of the piece.

The judge presiding over the case, a Mr. Justice Eve, felt that to rule in favor of Bond's defense would be to admit that ghosts were real, which he could not bring himself to do.

He decided that since Cummins was the one who had physically written the original document, she was entitled to ownership. From that point on, it was established that any works created during automatic writing sessions belong to the person doing the writing.

HISTORY OF PLANCHETTES

While now widely recognized as the tool used in conjunction with the Ouija board, the planchette was originally designed with automatic writing in mind!

A piece of lead is attached to one leg of the planchette, and then the fingertips of the participant(s) are placed along the edges of the device. It is then moved by a spirit, spelling out words and phrases.

Thanks to the work of planchette collectors and enthusiasts like Brandon Hodge, we know that the planchette originated in France on June 10, 1853, and that part of its first message in session was "I expressly forbid your repeating to anyone what I have just told you. The next time I write, I shall do it better."

In a book published in 1868, however, a man named G. W. Cottrell claimed that the planchette was originally created by a sect of French monks who used it in their monastery.

Regardless of how the planchette was created, it is quite interesting to see a connection between monks and automatic writing appear once again in a story.

HOW TO PRACTICE AUTOMATIC WRITING

1. As with all séances, you should follow the steps in chapter 5.

2. Gather your materials. This will include a notebook or large sheets of paper and pens, pencils, or paint. I strongly recommend that beginners use a large sheet of paper while developing their technique. Always have backup pages and writing utensils on hand. Nothing is worse than being in the middle of a session when your pencil breaks and there's no spare within reach.

3. You will want to make sure you are in a spot where you feel comfortable sitting for ten to thirty minutes. If you aren't comfortable, you will be distracted and fidgety, which can break you out of your trance.

4. When you're ready, hold your writing utensil to your paper. Don't begin writing yet: just become aware of how the writing implement feels in your hand.

5. Take that awareness and begin to apply it to the rest of your body. How do your toes feel? How about your shoulders? Lower back?

6. As you work on being present with your body, begin to take deep and mindful breaths.

7. Begin moving your hand. Keep contact with the paper. Move your hand up and down, left and right. Try scribbling or drawing circles.

8. Continue letting your body and mind relax. Resist the urge to look at what you are writing.

9. Your mind may begin to wander now. Let the thoughts flow in and out of your consciousness. Don't fight them: just acknowledge their presence and move on. If you are attempting to communicate with a specific spirit, you

GOODCHILD'S
EGYPTIAN BLACK INK
WRITES & REMAINS AN INTENSE BLACK
NEW YORK   TORONTO   LONDON, ENG

may find thinking of them helpful.

10. As different thoughts or feelings arise, you may notice your hand changing its movement or direction. You could be making big, loopy lines or small chicken scratch. During your first session, don't worry about where you are writing. Going over the same areas is fine. This session is all about learning to relax and letting your hand do what it wants.

11. When you notice your arm beginning to feel sore or tired, it is time to end the session. This could be after thirty seconds or thirty minutes. There is no correct time frame for automatic writing, but most people find that just a few minutes is plenty.

12. Put down your pencil and take a look at your sheets. What do you see? At first it will likely look like a big old mess, but don't get discouraged. Take your time looking over the sheets. Look for numbers, letters, and shapes.

13. Now (consciously) write down whatever you see in your notebook, even if that is nothing. Follow the worksheet on pages 146–47.

HELPFUL TIPS

If your first session was a smashing success, congratulations! But in case it wasn't, here are some tips to help you for next time.

- Use your nondominant hand for writing. As we cover in the tasseography chapter, your nondominant hand is believed to be your spirit hand or unconscious mind hand.
- Some people find a bit of distraction helpful. Try reading a book, talking on the phone, or listening to music while doing automatic writing. Your conscious mind will be focused on a task while your writing hand is free to move. The only downside to this method is that you may be influenced by what you are seeing and hearing.
- Take pictures of your papers. The cameras on our phones sometimes see

things that we don't.

- If you do happen to see an image or a word, you can use the tasseography dictionary to help you decipher the meaning of your markings.
- Try switching your writing utensil. If you tried with a pencil the first time, try using a marker or pen the next.
- Begin a daily meditation practice. This is helpful for all types of divination but especially automatic writing.
- Try moving your hand in conjunction with your exhales as you breathe.

RECORD KEEPING

Date:

Time:

People present:

Séance details (candles, heirlooms, etc.):

Spirits contacted:

Utensils used:

Symbols:

Words:

Phrases:

Notes:

8

Bibliomancy

WHAT IS BIBLIOMANCY?

It could be argued that books are the greatest of all human inventions. I don't say this as a writer but as a regular person whose life has been shaped by them.

Reading a book is seen as such a mundane thing, but it is actually a privilege to be able to read. For centuries, books were something that could be enjoyed by only the upper classes or certain community leaders. And while in most places books are now widely available, there are still 770 million people who are illiterate, the majority of them girls and women.

Whether we are looking at the very first religious scrolls in a museum or at an e-book we borrowed from the library, books have long given us the tools we need to solve life's mysteries...one page at a time.

Because of books' cultural impact, practicing bibliomancy is one of the most powerful forms of divination.

Bibliomancy, or stichomancy, simply means to divine (the future) from a book. For many centuries, it was done with religious or sacred texts like the Bible or the Torah, but these days any book can be used. Like all types of divination, bibliomancy has evolved for the modern world. It isn't just about predicting the future anymore; it's about gaining insight into all sorts of situations and also about spirit communication.

A question is asked and then a page or specific line is chosen and read to obtain the answer. Methods of choosing the passage vary, and can be as simple or as intricate as the inquirer would like. I will walk you through the most common method on pages 161–62.

BIBLIOMANCY HISTORY

The history of books and the history of bibliomancy are really one and the same.

Different cultures have practiced various forms of this divination for hundreds, if not thousands, of years. They have each contributed to the practice of divining from texts in their own way.

Mesopotamia

The earliest form of writing, known as cuneiform, is approximately six thousand years old, and it comes from the ancient civilization Mesopotamia (modern-day Iraq).

Invented by the Sumerians, cuneiform began as pictograms that depicted only nouns, but it eventually evolved to include all parts of speech.

What was the purpose of creating the first written language? Well, to document trade. That may not seem very exciting to us, but for society it was huge.

It is unknown whether writing was used in a divinatory capacity. Perhaps if Mesopotamia hadn't fallen, its people would have become the first bibliomancers.

Egypt

Between the years 4000 and 3001 BCE, the Ancient Egyptians began creating their hieroglyph language in order to communicate ideas.

By the year 2200 BCE, they were writing everything from instruction manuals to songs and even biographies of important people. Most of these works were written by scribes on rolls of papyrus, which is a plant-based paperlike material, but they can also be found on wooden planks and carved into stone.

The scribes were the rock stars of the Ancient Egyptian world. This elite group of people knew everything that went on in the kingdom, and nothing got done in government without one there to record it.

In a way, they were like a combination of modern-day elected officials and publishing houses.

If you were one of the scribes who specialized in religious affairs, you really had it made.

You see, everything pertaining to daily life was also a matter of religion, including various forms of divination.

These scribes would write out divinatory instructions step-by-step and recite them during rituals. Without the Ancient Egyptian influence on spiritual writing, this very book might not exist!

Mesoamerica

Despite there being many different Mesoamerican cultures spanning 2000 BCE to 1500 AD, it is definitely the Maya and their hieroglyphics that took center stage.

Divination was extremely important to the Mayans. Information relating to astrology and religion was recorded on the stones of temples and on plant fiber papers or animal skins. These collections of writings would also sometimes be protected with wooden covers.

Most people have heard of the Mayan calendar, or at the very least have heard the theory that the world would end on December 21, 2012. Thankfully, this prediction was incorrect, but anticipating the date's arrival did spark new conversations about Mayan culture.

The three main calendars of the Maya were complex and sophisticated, each designed to track and predict different things.

Unfortunately, knowledge of these divinatory systems was considered evil by the Spanish invaders, and sadly, many records were destroyed. The few surviving examples provide only a small glimpse at the extent of the Mayan belief systems.

China

While mass book production was just a twinkle in the eye of Western Europe, the Chinese were already masters of the art, and had been printing full-length texts for centuries using wooden blocks. In fact, China has been using types of ink presses since around the second century AD. It is safe to say that the first books (in the way we would recognize them today) were printed in China.

But how did written language and printing begin in China?

Well, they actually evolved from divination!

Oracle bones have been found by archaeologists around the country dating as far back as 1600 BCE, and it is believed that they were already a well-established method of divination by this date.

It is only natural that since writing and printing began with divination in China, divination would return to publishing as the process evolved. It is in China that we see one of the first forms of bibliomancy, performed using a sacred text known as the I Ching.

The I Ching is one of the oldest books on philosophical and spiritual thought in the history of the world. Its purpose is to provide wisdom and guidance throughout a person's life. Similar to tarot, the I Ching deals with archetypes. Situations are viewed and interpreted based on how they will progress.

Europe

Though many cultures have practiced forms of bibliomancy and recorded their divinatory practices in books, the method I am teaching you has its roots in European history.

We begin this journey with the Greeks and Romans.

The Ancient Greeks were an interesting civilization in that even though much of their lore, religion, and history was recorded on scrolls, they still preferred to share their history orally among themselves. Records were just something they felt they "had" to keep.

The practice of writing down ideas became fashionable during the Roman Empire, and during their many campaigns, the Romans brought their books with them. It was even common for upper-class Romans to build extensive libraries and show off their collections.

Like the Greeks, the Romans believed that everything was controlled by fate and the gods. Your path could be deciphered with divination, and considering their love of texts, it makes perfect sense that they would marry the two.

The two most common forms of bibliomancy for the Romans were Sortes Vergilianae and Sortes Homericae.

Sortes Vergilianae was performed by interpreting passages from the works of the Roman poet Virgil, who in later centuries was given an almost magical backstory and a larger-than-life reputation.

Sortes Homericae was performed by interpreting passages from the works of the Greek poet Homer. The text chosen most often seems to have been the *Iliad*, but the *Odyssey* would have been used as well.

The Romans believed that whatever line your eyes fell upon when you first looked at the page was the one you were meant to receive. From there, you would interpret the passage in a way that fit your circumstance. This could be by changing the verb tense or by replacing names with your own.

During the reign of the emperor Constantine from 306 to 337 AD, the Romans began converting to the new religion of Christianity and began working on compiling religious texts and ideas.

After the fall of the Roman Empire in the fifth century, large areas of Europe came up for grabs, and invasion after invasion swept the continent.

It's during this period that books found safe harbor in monasteries.

Monks not only protected these texts but copied them for their own personal collections. This was more than a way to pass the time; it was a sacred duty.

Throughout the Middle Ages, the Bible would be used by people to predict the future—though this was not a common practice and was outwardly forbidden by the church.

It makes sense that the Bible would be the default tool for bibliomancy. Not only did religion play a massive role in daily life, but the Bible was a book that everyone knew and community leaders had access to.

However, in the fifteenth century, one man would change the landscape of books, and therefore the art of bibliomancy, forever.

Johannes Gutenberg was a German inventor and goldsmith who created the first printing press that used movable type.

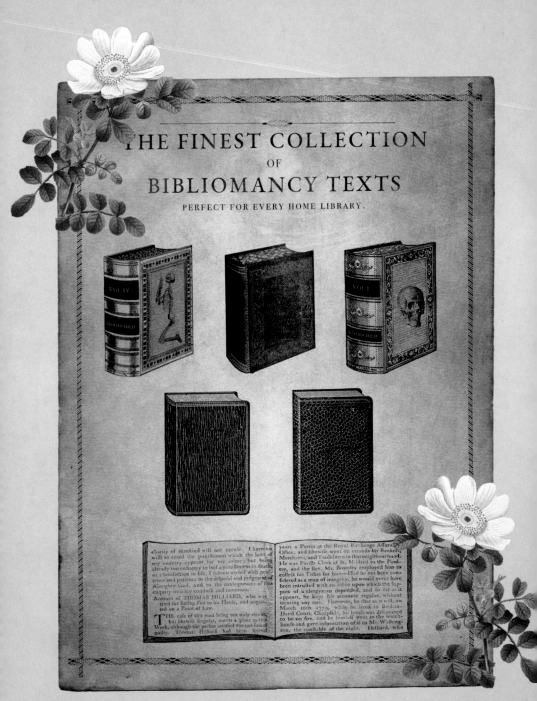

Europeans had already been using woodblock printing presses, but this was time-consuming and expensive. With Gutenberg's invention, mass production and more affordable texts became a reality. Books were no longer something possessed by a handful of select religious individuals or government workers.

This quite literally brought us into the period known as the Renaissance. As books and ideas spread, philosophy, art, and literature were once again held in high regard.

By the Victorian era, more and more people saw value in the ability to read and write. Parents who could afford it would send their children to school earlier in life as well as for longer, though this was generally still something reserved for male offspring.

The rise of spiritualism in the late nineteenth century and secularism's popularity in the twentieth century meant that bibliomancy was due for a change during this time too.

The Bible was a bit passé, so beloved novels and poems were given new life as divinatory texts. These books could now entertain you *and* provide important messages from the spirit world.

Bibliomancy as we practice it today was born.

Folklore

Because many of us use bibliomancy to seek answers and uncover various truths to improve our lives, we must recognize that there have been periods of time when bibliomancy was used to hurt and punish people.

Both in medieval and early modern Europe, there were countless waves of witch executions. These hunts primarily affected women, usually ones who were outspoken or had broken free from gender norms.

Religious texts and witch-hunting instruction manuals were used to justify the unthinkable torture these women endured.

Despite the church's disapproval, various types of divination were still quite common throughout Europe and practiced by all sorts of people, including the clergy themselves.

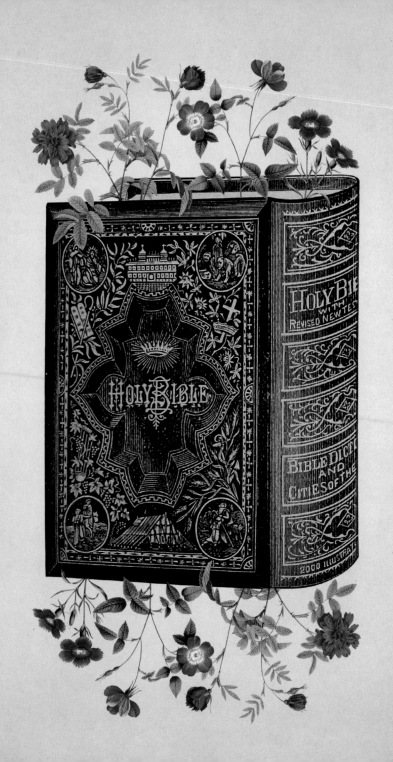

Witch weighing

One rather crude form of bibliomancy, performed by the church and not an actual recognized legal process, involved weighing an accused witch against a Bible. It was thought that if the woman weighed more than the Bible, she was innocent. In some records, it is the reverse that determines guilt. It goes to show that these women were essentially set up to fail from the start. (It should be noted that during the sixteenth and seventeenth centuries, church Bibles were huge, heavy things, sometimes weighing over a hundred pounds, and therefore could be used in this manner.)

But it wasn't just the physical weight of the book that was important.

Bibles were seen as containing universal truths about what was moral and good. The words housed within them were that of God himself, and a witch surely could not measure up against something so powerful.

The belief surrounding the word of God still holds true today.

People often recite passages during moments of fear in order to expel "evil" from their surroundings or to protect themselves.

If you do a search online for ways to rid your house of a negative spirit or entity, there is no shortage of websites that suggest incorporating Bible verses into your ritual.

Key and Bible

Have you ever played spin the bottle? If you haven't, it goes something like this. A group of teens sits in a circle with an empty glass bottle (generally a wine bottle) on its side in the center. One person then spins the bottle, and whomever the mouth points to has to kiss the spinner.

Well, there was a time when this same concept was supposedly used not to determine whom to kiss…but rather to determine who was guilty of a crime.

Various suspects would be seated at a table in a circle.

Next, a Bible would be placed in the center, with a key on top of it.

The key would be spun, and whomever it was pointing at when it stopped was the guilty party.

I find divination incredibly useful for navigating areas of my life, but I am also happy it is no longer used in the justice system.

PERFORMING A READING/DOING BIBLIOMANCY

Choosing a book

Choosing the correct book to perform your reading is the most important part of bibliomancy.

Your choice will contribute to the context, tone, and overall mood of your reading.

If you are attempting to communicate with the spirit of your great-grandfather who was a bit of a practical joker, a humorous novel may be the right choice, but the same cannot be said when you're making inquiries surrounding your career...unless, of course, you happen to be a stand-up comedian.

Subject matter

Whether it be a religious book or a vampire novel, choose an appropriate subject for your reading.

Dictionaries of all sorts can make wonderful bibliomancy tools. A dream dictionary can unlock an entire world of symbolism, and an *Oxford English Dictionary* can help expand your vocabulary in new ways.

If you are doing a reading about eliminating debt, a book on financial literacy may be just what you need.

TIP: Try using this book when performing spirit-focused bibliomancy!

Familiarity

Most people have a favorite book they return to time and time again. Using a story you know can add an element of comfort and understanding to your reading.

The downside to this is that sometimes we know a book so well we subconsciously turn to a specific page or passage that aligns with the answer we want to receive, rather than the one we need to receive.

Sentimentality

Just as you have a favorite book, there is a good chance your ancestors did as well. If your mother loved *Alice's Adventures in Wonderland* when she was a child, that could be the perfect book to use when communicating with her spirit.

Cover

If you are a visual person, it might be in your best interest to judge a book by its cover. Different shapes and images can add a level of depth to your reading.

Not only that, but color has been shown to influence your mood and is used to help convey messages subconsciously.

> TIP: Try using the candle color chart on page 76 to help you pick a book based on color!

Condition and binding

When the book we are called to use is in a fragile or compromised state, it is best to choose a different one, especially if the book is old or a special edition.

Always inspect the book thoroughly, even if it is brand-new. Sometimes the spine is cracked or the pages are bound in specific spots, and what we believe is a spirit guiding us is actually just the result of strategic glue and thread placement.

Instructions

1. Once you have chosen your book, it is time to begin your séance. Follow the steps in chapter 5 on how to begin!

2. If you are just seeking general advice about a situation, then lay the book in front of you and spend a few moments thinking about all the people over the centuries who made this moment possible. Think about the writers, the inventors, even think about the person who delivered the ink to the printer that created the markings that now adorn the pages.

3. If you are attempting to communicate with a specific spirit, lay the book in front of you and spend a few moments thinking about that person. Think of their accomplishments, think of their laugh, or think of your favorite memory with them.

4. When you feel connected, you will want to pick up the book. Run your hands over the cover and the pages. Notice how the book feels. Is it heavy? Do the pages stick together? You may find it helpful to repeat your question out loud during this time.

5. When you're ready, choose a page of the book for your answer. Let your intuition guide you to the right one and flip the book open.

6. You can either read the first passage or line that your eyes fall upon or you can try closing your eyes and running your finger across the page until you feel you should stop. This is your answer. Your message could be contained in one line, one paragraph, or even the entire page. Follow your intuition.

7. You have now completed your reading! You can repeat this process as many times as needed. Close your séance and be sure to fill out the worksheet on pages 164–65.

TIP: Bibliomancy, while quite easy to perform, isn't always easy to interpret. There isn't a list of set meanings to work from like there is in tasseography or tarot. The answers you receive aren't always straightforward. If you are struggling to understand a message, write it down and review it at another time. What doesn't make sense today may make perfect sense tomorrow!

MODERNIZING BIBLIOMANCY

The world we live in is full of amazing technology that can be utilized to enhance divination and put a new spin on age-old practices. Try incorporating the following ideas into your session.

Use a random number generator to choose a page to read from.

Number generators are easy to find online. All you need to do is type in the number of pages your book has, and the generator will choose one for you.

You can narrow this down further by counting the paragraphs on the page and using the generator again to decide which one to read.

Use the search feature that comes with most e-readers.

I like to meditate for a few minutes until a word, image, or phrase comes to my mind. When I have settled on one, I open my e-reader, choose a book, and use the search function to look for the word (or image or phrase) within it.

RECORD KEEPING

Date:

Time:

People present:

Séance details (candles, heirlooms, etc.):

Spirit contacted:

Questions asked:

Book used:

Page number:

Line or paragraph:

Notes:

9

Spirit Board

WHAT IS A SPIRIT BOARD?

Of all the tools created for spirit communication and divination, the spirit board is the most famous, the most feared, and the most misunderstood.

Most people outside the paranormal or occult community don't know what a spirit board is until you say the name Ouija, and then they know exactly what you are referring to.

Their looks of apprehension are usually coupled with remarks about evil, or a story that happened to a friend of a friend who played with the board.

A spirit board, which is also known as a talking board, is a thin, flat plank with letters and numbers printed on it. Usually this is accompanied with the words "Yes," "No," and "Goodbye."

While originally crafted with wood, these days most spirit boards are made of heavy cardboard or particleboard. It turns out that not even spirit tools can escape the cost-cutting practices of capitalism.

Using a spirit board is a form of channeling. The participants of a séance place their fingers on a planchette, a teardrop- or heart-shaped piece of wood or plastic with a circular window in its center, and it moves around the board, compelled by a spirit, spelling out words.

As I discussed on page 141, planchettes were originally created for use in automatic writing, another form of spirit channeling.

SPIRIT BOARD HISTORY

Writing about spirit board history is tricky, as there is no one true origin story. Multiple devices were invented in the mid- to late nineteenth century that acted as precursors of this idea. The most obvious evolution of the spirit board is that it stems from automatic writing. This is why we see the planchette modified to work on the board.

Spirit boards became a cost-efficient and quick way to contact the dead. It was convenient, because you no longer had to hire a medium to provide you with messages or wait around for hours counting out spirit rappings.

While there is no definitive, straightforward answer to the question of who created the first spirit board, lucky for us, the brand Ouija comes with a timeline that most historians and enthusiasts agree is sound.

In 1891, ads began appearing in newspapers like the *Toronto Star* and the *Baltimore Sun* that read:

OUIJA!

The Mysterious Talking Board

Fun, Mystery, and Instruction for the Home Circle and Evening Parties.

Everyone has one but you, and if you see it work once, you'll have one too.

PRICE: $1.50 COMPLETE

TALKING BOARDS

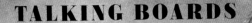

OUIJA

YES   NO

A B C D E F G H I J K L M
N O P Q R S T U V W X Y Z
1 2 3 4 5 6 7 8 9 0

GOODBYE

THE NEW GAME
MANUFACTURED BY
The Kennard Novelty Co.,

OUIJA

(TRADE-MAR

PRONOUNCED WE-JA

The Egyptian Luck B
A Talking Board.

*Most Wonderful Invention
of the 19th Century.*

THIS WONDERFUL TALKING BOARD!
ONLY $1.99 AT TOWNSEND GAMES

MYSTIFYING
ORACLE   NO

A C D E F G H I J K L M
N O P Q R S T U V W X Y Z
1 2 3 4 5 6 7 8 9 0

GOOD BYE

The public went crazy for these mysterious boards, and soon it was hard to find a household that didn't have one of their own.

But how did this craze start?

In October 1890, a group of men—Charles W. Kennard, Harry Welles Rusk, William H. A. Maupin, Colonel Washington Bowie, and John F. Green—decided to go into business together and created the Kennard Novelty Company.

These men were not spiritualists but rather intelligent investors who decided to capitalize on the popularity of the spiritualism movement.

Their first Ouija design was brought to the patent board by a lawyer named Elijah Bond in late 1890, and in February 1891 the company was awarded its patent.

This was also the first time the Ouija was seen as a game instead of a spirit communication device.

The main theory I have seen surrounding the decision to deem Ouija a game is that the Kennard Novelty Company would have had lower patent fees or taxes on a game than on a tool—that, and it was incumbent on the company to prove to the patent office that the device actually worked. If you ask any paranormal investigator, they will tell you it is easier to present an occult specialty item as a toy rather than try to prove definitively that ghosts are real.

The Kennard Novelty Company wasn't the first company to start producing spirit boards, but it was the first to get the design and the marketing just right.

All entrepreneurs know that having your product take off involves more than just a great idea. Everything from luck to timing to image plays a massive role in success.

In late 1891, Kennard and Maupin sold their interest in the company. Whether this was by choice remains to be seen.

From there, Bowie and Rusk took control and restructured the company.

In an unpredictable move, they placed their employee and friend William Fuld in charge of operations.

Whatever the reason for this decision, it turned out to be a good one.

William Fuld was a strategic leader, and in 1892, he rebranded the Kennard Novelty Company the Ouija Novelty Company.

Under his leadership, sales of the boards took off; soon many imitators were attempting to re-create the magic with their own designs, including some variations by none other than Charles Kennard (though unfortunately they never took off).

William Fuld aggressively went after these imitators, one of whom was his own brother. In 1901, Isaac Fuld produced his own board, and the brothers' feud reached its boiling point. Because of this rift, the two sides of the family did not speak for ninety-six years! Isaac went as far as having his deceased daughter's body exhumed and removed from the family plot to be buried elsewhere.

Over the years, William Fuld trademarked various phrases surrounding the board, including an Egyptian luck board (at the time, Egyptomania was having a resurgence in the West). This move surely boosted sales but has contributed greatly to Ouija fakelore that has been hard to undo and move past.

Though Ouija was already affordable, the company also created a budget-friendly version called the Mystifying Oracle. If you own a modern Ouija board, you may notice that this phrase is now used as a tagline of sorts.

Then, in 1919, the direction of William Fuld's life would change forever.

The story goes that Fuld was told by his Ouija board to "prepare for big business," a sign he took to mean he should go ahead with his plan to build a bigger warehouse.

A few years later, in 1927, near the end of construction, Fuld was overseeing the placing of a flag on the roof of the building when the barrier fence he was holding broke loose and he fell to the ground.

Though his injuries did ultimately prove fatal, he lived long enough to tell his relatives to never sell Ouija to anyone outside the family.

They kept their word until 1966, when the Parker brothers gave them an offer they could not refuse.

The Parker brothers decided to keep the spookiness-driven marketing that Fuld had crafted so well.

Since Parker Brothers was founded in Salem, Massachusetts, the company began to claim that the boards were actually manufactured there, playing up the mystical associations attached to the area.

The box for the Ouija boards designed in the 1960s shows a shrouded figure covering his face and waving his hand. It looks as if he is casting a spell in order to move the planchette from the great beyond...and one does wonder if this ghostly figure is an homage to William Fuld, whose name was left on the box. Perhaps this had been part of the sales terms, or maybe it was because the story of his death enhanced the board's spooky reputation.

The purchase of Ouija by Parker Brothers turned out to be a great business move, as interest in spiritualism surged during the birth of the New Age movement.

Peace, love, and bodily autonomy were the order of the day, and the only demons people faced were their own. Ghosts were once again seen as welcome companions to the living, much as they had been in the Victorian and Edwardian eras.

Then, in the late 1970s and early '80s, spiritualism, and therefore Ouija boards, would be dealt a major blow.

This blow wasn't in sales but in terms of reputation.

Fundamentalist Christian groups in North America and parts of Europe had been denouncing modern spiritualism for quite a while, but their attention zeroed in on Ouija after the release of the wildly popular book and horror film *The Exorcist*.

In this story, the main character—Linda Blair in the film—plays with a Ouija board and becomes possessed by a demon.

And while *The Exorcist* is ultimately a metaphor about the battle of good versus evil that is thought to exist in all of us, this unfortunate portrayal of Ouija has left the board riddled with negative connotations and tainted by misinformation.

Nevertheless, Parker Brothers didn't let this association with evil discourage them and even used it to their advantage to sell boards.

During the Satanic Panic of the 1980s (a movement—backed by the church—that spread conspiracy theories of satanic cults roaming the United States, looking to infiltrate homes and harm children), the company began marketing the Ouija as a thing rebellious teens could do at sleepovers and Friday night parties.

Then, in 1991, Hasbro purchased Parker Brothers, including the best-selling spirit board.

Hasbro decided to play up the divination aspect of the board, marketing it more as a fortune-telling device akin to a Magic 8-Ball.

They ran a series of commercials featuring two boys using the Ouija. Questions like "Will tomorrow be a snow day?" and "Will I ever be tall enough to slam-dunk?" flashed across the screen.

While all divinatory tools are used for predictions, this was the first time Ouija was advertised without its spooky and spiritualist origins. The boys treat the board as a fun, lighthearted game.

One thing that cannot be ignored when looking back on this history is that most adults who have a negative view or scary stories associated with the board were children in the 1970s, '80s, and early '90s.

Kids tend to embellish, and those experiences can feel very real (and were of course real to the participants), but they aren't the most reliable source.

Not only that, but it is a common belief in the paranormal world that children are more susceptible to the paranormal.

It definitely makes for a case against children using divinatory tools unless supervised by adults who are well versed in the practice.

Since acquiring Ouija, Hasbro has faced numerous protests by religious groups that denounce the board as a gateway or portal to evil.

These leftover feelings and beliefs stemming from the Satanic Panic are held as a universal truth by the majority of people, despite Ouija's clever marketing throughout various "ages of misinformation."

Even I haven't been immune to some of these beliefs, and was sometimes nervous around spirit boards despite owning many of them. It wasn't until I did my research that I fully understood the potential of this divinatory tool.

As the early spiritualists believed, these boards have the ability to provide incredible messages from ghosts and spirits.

Like all items used for connecting with the dead, spirit boards require our respect and need to be approached with the proper mindset and boundaries in place. But they also deserve our admiration instead of a false reputation.

They really are no different from any other spirit communication tool.

Fun facts about Ouija

Elijah Bond's headstone is engraved with a Ouija design!

William Fuld was known as the man with the most patents. At one point he even created a "Ouija oil," which was a treatment for colds and flus.

POPULAR OUIJA BELIEFS AND SUPERSTITIONS

In this age of the internet, many of the superstitions about spirit boards that took hold in the 1970s and '80s have been able to run rampant unchecked. Everyone from the church to witchcraft practitioners to paranormal investigators has had a hand in perpetuating these ideas.

I have compiled a list of the most popular Ouija superstitions, in no specific order. Some of them raise a good point, while others are just, well…superstitions.

1. Do not use a spirit board in your own home.

The thought behind this is that you will open a door in your home to evil entities. This generally overlooks the fact that millions of boards have been sold since their creation, the majority of which have been used in the owners' homes.

2. Don't ask inappropriate questions or make jokes.

This is actually a good rule of thumb for any form of spirit communication. Always maintain a level of seriousness and respect when speaking with the dead.

3. It is bad luck to leave the planchette on the board when you have finished your session.

Cleaning and storing your tools properly is something you should do every time you use them. See chapter 15, "Caring for Your Tools," for tips.

4. You should always say goodbye when you have finished a session; otherwise you are leaving the doorway you created to the spirit realm open.

This is a good practice for any séance, if for no other reason than it is polite and respectful.

5. If the spirit begins counting down the numbers or going backward through the alphabet, this means an evil spirit is trying to "leave the board."

From my experience, if a spirit wants to manifest, they will; they don't need a spirit board to do it. Physical manifestations are considered to be quite rare, and if every time the spirit board counted down meant there was an evil spirit or demon running around, we would have quite the problem on our hands.

Using divinatory tools for spirit communication is about creating a focal point or spiritual anchor for communication between the living and the dead. It is a method to speak to each other in a way we both can understand. These items don't grant extra powers to a spirit that they wouldn't already have.

Of course, an argument can be made that putting your energy into the object allows for a spirit to draw upon it and manipulate it, so maybe in a way there is something to this one...

You be the judge.

6. Don't use a spirit board in a cemetery.

Again, this isn't terrible advice. Cemeteries are magical and sacred places, but if you are brand-new to divination, you may want to wait until you have some sessions under your belt and know how to maintain energetic boundaries before using a spirit board in a hypercharged place.

7. Don't use the board alone.

While it's a bit trickier, practically speaking, to use a spirit board alone, it is not inherently more dangerous to do so.

8. Don't use spirit boards as home decor or jewelry.

I believe you can respectfully incorporate spirit board designs into other objects. These boards are aesthetically pleasing and their art should be appreciated. In fact, William Fuld, the head of the Ouija Novelty Company, agreed and created his own line of Ouija jewelry.

PARALLELS TO TAROT CARDS

Though totally different tools, tarot and spirit boards have some interesting connections that should be noted.

1. Tarot began as a game and evolved into a divinatory tool, and the spirit board began as a divinatory tool and evolved into a game.

2. A lot of the same rumors that haunt spirit boards are also applied to tarot, namely that they are both objects that can be manipulated by demons. However, these beliefs don't seem to have become attached to tarot in the same way. Could this be another result of the Ouija Satanic Panic?

3. Both tarot and spirit boards were given Egyptian fakelore backstories to make them seem more mythical or magical to the average consumer.

HOW DID OUIJA GET ITS NAME?

While we may never know the truth surrounding this question, there are two popular theories that are worth sharing.

1. The Ouija is a combination of the French word *oui* and the German word *ja*, both of which mean yes.

2. The second theory is that Helen, the sister-in-law of Elijah Bond, worked as a medium and provided the name. While in a session together, the group

asked the board what it wanted its name to be, and it replied with the letters o-u-i-j-a. When they asked what the board meant, it responded with the letters g-o-o-d l-u-c-k. However, Helen was known to wear a locket that had a portrait of a woman with the name Ouida spelled out on it. Ouida was the pseudonym of the English novelist Maria Louise Ramé. Perhaps whoever (or whatever) was moving the planchette simply misread the name?

PARANORMAL STORY: SETH SPEAKS

> In order to combat some of the negativity that surrounds the spirit board, I have opted not to include any of the scary stories involving them. Instead, I want to tell you about a fascinating woman who played a pivotal role in shaping the New Age movement.

Dorothy Jane Roberts, who went by Jane, was born in New York State in spring 1929.

Her parents divorced when she was quite young, and her mother, Marie, moved the two of them into the home of Marie's parents, where the small family barely scraped by financially.

Marie suffered from a debilitating case of rheumatoid arthritis, and Jane spent most of her childhood caring for her bedridden mother. Not only was this a lot of pressure on the young girl, but Marie would often berate and ridicule her daughter, resulting in Jane's low self-esteem.

Eventually the state stepped in, and Jane was moved to an orphanage run by Catholic nuns. Her mother had been transferred to a hospital for proper care, and Marie's father, while supportive, just couldn't care for Jane financially.

Religion seemed to offer Jane hope and something to believe in, but after the death of her grandfather when she was nineteen, her passions turned toward writing and science.

Jane went on to create works encompassing a broad range of subjects, from science fiction to children's stories.

In 1954, Jane married a man named Robert Butts, and the pair eventually moved to Elmira, New York. It was there in Elmira, in 1963, that Jane began researching the concept of extrasensory perception.

Extrasensory perception, or ESP, is the ability to obtain knowledge from sources, such as other people, telepathically or in ways that are outside the scope of the five human senses.

Jane decided that to further her research, she and her husband, Rob, would experiment with a Ouija board.

It wasn't long before the pair began receiving messages from a spirit whom Jane called Seth.

The woman and the spirit would go on to develop a very close relationship, with Seth providing answers to many of the big universal questions.

He explained concepts like reincarnation and past lives and gave insight into different entities, such as angels that exist in the world, all via the Ouija board.

Seth even coined the popular New Age phrase "You create your own reality."

Eventually, Jane began hearing Seth's thoughts directly inside her mind and was able to channel his spirit without the aid of the Ouija board.

Oddly enough, it was Jane herself who showed the most skepticism toward Seth. She often wondered if he was just a part of herself.

Nevertheless, Jane and Rob would go on to publish books of Seth's ideas and teachings.

Unfortunately, the health problems that plagued Jane's mother would come to take her life as well in 1984, after she had become bedridden and endured several long hospital stays.

Rob devoted the rest of his life to promoting and organizing Jane's work. It was a thoughtful tribute to the person he loved most, and it's lucky for us he did it, as there is a lot we can learn from Jane and Seth.

USING A SPIRIT BOARD

There are two main ways to use a spirit board: in a group or alone. Both are effective, though group sessions can yield more consistent results.

In a group

This is the traditional way to use the board, and generally the more effective of the two.

It is vitally important that all people involved share an understanding of the board, including its history.

Everyone should be in a positive mindset, and each person should have one or two spirits in mind that they would like to communicate with. Each person should also provide the spirits' names and a rough outline of questions for both the leader and the record keeper. For example, if you have a group of three sitters in the séance, you will generate a list of six names. The record keeper will go through the list of names one by one during the session, and everyone will be asked to focus on that individual.

Unless you are experienced, I don't recommend asking just any spirit to join you. I believe this is a good practice for all forms of divination, but with spirit boards, it is especially easy to let negative associations into your consciousness.

Each person will be assigned a role in the group.

The first is known as the leader. This person will be the one who asks the questions and calls out the letters that are provided by the spirit; the record keeper jots them down. During the séance, the leader should be the only one who speaks.

The record keeper does not actively participate with the board, but rather takes notes on the questions asked and all the answers or messages obtained from the session.

The sitters are the remaining participants who sit around the board with their fingers on the planchette (the leader also touches the planchette). It is best to limit your sitters to two or three, as any more and it can be a little bit crowded.

Though the roles are generally decided ahead of the séance, you may find it helpful to switch things up mid-séance for better results.

Instructions

1. Once roles have been assigned and the record keeper is ready, you can begin the séance. Be sure to follow the steps in chapter 5 and set clear boundaries.

2. The leader should be seated at the bottom of the board, with the widest part of the planchette in front of them, planchette legs on the board and the pointed end facing toward the letters.

3. The leader and sitters should now place two fingers from their nondominant hand on the planchette. Most people find the index and middle fingers to be the most comfortable fit.

4. When the leader is ready, that person can say "Hello" and explain out loud the purpose of the séance and then begin asking questions. Because everyone should have provided the names of spirits they want to speak to in advance, the leader should have the order of communication ready. The leader can now invite the first spirit to join the séance.

5. After the first question, the planchette may or may not move. After you have provided adequate time for a response, the leader can move on.

6. After all the questions have been asked (and hopefully answered), it is time to end the séance.

7. All participants should thank the spirits for their time and say goodbye. As a group you may also slide the planchette across to the "Goodbye" printed on the board if you see fit.

8. Once you have closed the session, you may find it beneficial to discuss the results. Each participant may want to copy the log kept by the record keeper and fill out the worksheet on pages 182–83.

By yourself

Working with a spirit board alone is very much like participating in an automatic writing session. It takes focus and determination but is entirely possible to do!

The steps are essentially the same as they are for "In a group," the only difference being that you are taking on all the roles.

Because you are the leader, sitter, and record keeper, you will want to incorporate a voice recorder into the mix.

During the séance, you will ask all your questions and say all the letters received out loud, while you use your intuition to move the planchette around the board.

Because you are recording everything, you won't be taken out of the moment in order to write things down or decipher the answers in depth.

There is one drawback to using the spirit board alone, however. Because you are doing all the tasks, this doesn't leave much room for a conversation. Going it alone is more like conducting an interview, and for this reason you should have a list of yes or no questions next to you before you begin.

Tips

- Though I have stressed this multiple times throughout the book, I'll say it again: a positive mindset is the most important aspect of spirit communication, and with spirit boards it is extra important.
- Don't ask frivolous questions unless you know that the spirit you are communicating with would be fine with it.
- Cleanse the board often. All divinatory tools need to be energetically cleansed, but with all the negative associations and urban legends attached to the boards, they need more than the average tool.
- Don't go looking for trouble—you just might find it!
- And most importantly, if you don't feel comfortable using a spirit board, then don't use it. There is no rule that says you have to use it just because the opportunity is there.

RECORD KEEPING

Date:

Time:

People present and roles performed:

Location:

Séance details (candles, heirlooms, etc.):

Spirits contacted:

Questions and responses:

Notes:

10

Tasseography

WHAT IS TASSEOGRAPHY?

Every time you sit down and pour yourself a cup of tea, you are participating in a sacred act that has been performed for thousands of years.

Whether you are taking part in a Japanese tea ceremony or just sipping some Earl Grey after a long day, the act of preparing and then drinking the tea is an important ritual.

Tasseography, or tasseomancy, is the conscious act of divining the future or reading spirit messages in the form of images left behind in a cup by loose tea leaves. The interpretation of these images in cups is a beautiful dance between the reader and the spirit. The reader takes the symbols that appear and tells the story the spirit needs to share.

Tea leaf reading is basically a type of scrying, but due to its complexity and large number of practitioners, it is in a category all its own.

A BRIEF HISTORY OF TASSEOGRAPHY

The practice of tasseography originally comes from Turkey, where instead of reading tea leaves, they read coffee grounds. This had been a well-established practice for hundreds of years due to the special relationship between the beverage and the drinker.

It was only natural that when tea became the drink of choice in the Western world, the existing divinatory systems would be altered to fit the new medium.

During the Victorian era, tea leaf reading was a popular social pastime for women, and it seems to have gained a significant foothold in both the highlands and lowlands of Scotland. Many of the meanings in the dictionary portion of this chapter were actually established during this period.

If you are interested in learning more, a book called *Tea-Cup Reading and the Art of Fortune-Telling by Tea Leaves* was written by "a Highland Seer" in 1881, and it's still considered a staple in learning the practice.

In order to truly understand tea leaf reading, we must look at the origins of drinking tea.

This important relationship humans have formed with tea began in China around five thousand years ago, and the story is affectionately retold through the following folktale.

Once upon a time, there lived a divine farmer named Shennong.

Shennong spent his days researching the plants and herbs of the region. The people of China were facing illness and famine, and he wanted to help them. As he was conducting his experiments, he happened to poison himself over seventy times.

Luckily, before the poison could take hold and kill him, the wind blew a tea leaf into the cup of water he was drinking.

The concoction healed Shennong, and he would go on to bring the knowledge of the magical and healing properties of tea to the people.

Mythology aside, people really have been using tea leaves in China for thousands of years, as supported by archaeological evidence. But the leaves were originally chewed or eaten for their benefits. It wasn't until fifteen hundred years ago that the leaves were brewed in hot water.

The creation of tea changed both the landscape and the ceremonial customs of China forever.

The use of tea quickly spread to surrounding areas, including Japan, which developed its own complex and beautiful ceremonies for tea.

Eventually China switched from using matcha, which is a powdered green tea, to dried loose-leaf tea and experimented with flavors and different strength profiles. China's expertise solidified its monopoly on the tea trade and allowed it to become an economic powerhouse.

In the early 1600s, Dutch traders brought tea to Europe. It exploded in popularity in Britain when Catherine of Braganza, who loved tea, married King Charles II.

This new passion for tea took hold right as Great Britain was becoming a world superpower, and its quest for dominating the tea market eventually led to the Opium Wars between Britain and China. Eventually the British Army defeated the armies of China in the 1800s and took control of the ship ports in Hong Kong for many years. China reluctantly began trading tea again.

Despite the many trade wars and years of bloodshed, tea has secured its spot as the second most consumed beverage on earth, after water.

Art would sometimes be drawn in the cup using the delicate foam of matcha, and while that is reminiscent of today's latte art, it also sparks a deep connection to tasseography.

TEA FOLKLORE

Not all folklore about tea is directly related to tasseography, but it is valuable knowledge to have in case you would like to incorporate some of these ideas into your practice.

- It is believed that if you throw your used tea leaves on a burning fire, you will drive poverty and bad luck away from your home.
- Accidentally spilling tea leaves inside your home when preparing a cup is a sign of good luck coming toward you.

- Intentionally spreading tea leaves outside your front door is thought to protect against negative spirits.
- English sailors were known to never empty their teapot when out at sea as it was believed that doing so was symbolic of "pouring out" their catch. Even stranger was that their families at home would not empty their own pots on the day the men set sail because they believed this would prevent the ship from sinking.
- If women were drinking tea together and one wanted to have a baby, she would declare her intention out loud and then be the one to pour the tea for the group.

PARANORMAL ENCOUNTER

As I began to do the research for this chapter, I decided it was time to use one of the teacups my nana had collected for my readings. Earlier in the book, I talked about how certain types of divination would come easily to you while others would take more time. Tasseography does not come naturally for me, so I knew that in order to get accurate spirit messages, I needed all the help I could get.

My nana didn't have much money, and the few china pieces she had acquired over the years were incredibly important to her.

When I was a child, I would take mental notes on each one. They were all from different sets, presumably abandoned at thrift stores or given to her as gifts. Most were decorated with small roses, which was both her favorite flower and a nod to her middle name, while others were painted with gold trim and small leaves.

The pieces looked to me like little porcelain castaways, carefully adopted and arranged perfectly in the wooden cabinet behind her sofa.

When my nana died, her collection was divided up between my father and his brother, and while the pieces remained cherished, they were also unused.

I had been attempting tasseography for years, and my readings up until that point had left me feeling confused. But instead of throwing in the tea towel, I decided to change my approach.

This is when I turned to my nana. I knew she would be receptive to communicating with me in this way, at least until I was ready to branch out. I also knew the teacups she cherished would have her energy attached to them.

Up until this point, I had been using a specialized tasseography teacup with symbols painted inside it to enhance the reading. (This can be very handy, but if you're already struggling to interpret the messages properly, these extra designs can hinder more than help.)

So there I was, once again scanning the display shelf of teacups, though now in my parents' kitchen, mulling over which would be the right one to begin with.

While your intuition is the most important aspect of picking a cup to work with, there are some other requirements to consider when it comes to tasseography, like size and shape. Don't worry: I go over these later in the chapter.

In the end I felt drawn to one of the gold-painted cups and brought it home with me to sit on my ancestor altar (see page 67) for a few days in order to draw my nana's energy into my space.

The next change I needed to make was the type of tea I was using.

Because my nana was a second-generation Canadian and strongly felt the influence of her British heritage, it seemed appropriate to use an English breakfast tea for my readings.

My choice to change the tea shows the importance of selecting your tools with intention and care. In terms of tea leaf reading, you're actually ingesting some of it into your body. By taking in something you know the spirit liked, you're strengthening your connection to the spirit.

That doesn't mean you can't choose your tea based on taste preference; one could also argue that this is the most important aspect of successful tasseography. But if you're looking to connect with a specific person, using tools that tie to their identity can really help.

Armed with my new supplies and a renewed sense of confidence, I picked a quiet afternoon to perform a session.

I poured my tea, lit a candle, and asked my nana to let me know if I was on the right track. As I sipped my tea, I noticed that I felt more relaxed. The pressure of trying to see images was no longer the most important thing. It was as if the point of the reading was to connect with her and enjoy the process of it all.

When it came time to flip my cup over, I felt calm and assured that whatever I did (or didn't) see was how it was meant to be.

As I peered into the teacup, there was no question about what was there.

A large rose looked back at me from the bottom of the cup. To its right was a small cluster of leaves that had formed into the shape of a heart.

I have made huge strides in my tea leaf reading since then. Of course, I still have days when I struggle to see the full picture, but my tasseography sessions are now also the time I get to spend with my nana, and that makes them valuable beyond measure.

Will the appearance of these two symbols convince a skeptic that the paranormal is real? Probably not, but that's the thing about divination and spirit communication: it's a very personal experience. The choice to believe is yours and yours alone.

If your goal is to prove the existence of ghosts to others, you may be performing thankless labor and might want to reconsider doing so.

And as you can see, some otherworldly experiences are simple. It isn't always an earth-shattering sign from the heavens, but rather something ordinary yet meaningful just to get you back on track.

HOW TO PERFORM TASSEOGRAPHY

Choosing a cup

The first step in learning tasseography is choosing an appropriate teacup to read from. Remember that this isn't just a vessel for holding liquid: it is also a divinatory tool. Its selection should be a part of the overall ritual.

1. **Size and shape:** While the amount of liquid your teacup holds is up to you, you do need to make sure the rim is wider than the bottom of the cup—called the well—in order to have a clear view of the leaves from all sides and angles. The saucer should also be wider than the cup by at least a few centimeters so when you flip the cup over, tea remnants have a place to go. The

interior of the cup should have no ridges or carvings that could potentially interfere with the leaves' distribution.

2. **Color:** Different colors can enhance your mood and add an interesting element to your reading, but it is best to begin with a plain white cup and saucer. If patterns and designs are featured, make sure they are confined to the outside of the cup. If you do go with a color, it should be light enough that you can still see the leaves clearly.

3. **Accessories:** One often overlooked part of tasseography is the use of a teaspoon. Not only do you need something to physically add tea to the cup, but it is considered bad luck to stir with anything other than a spoon. Because teaspoons are a common collectible, you will be able to find a wide variety of them. This is a place where you can bring different energy into your reading by incorporating different designs and patterns.

   Using a teaspoon with a heart on the handle can be reserved for love readings. A decorative travel spoon from Japan can connect you to your great-grandfather who lived there.

4. **A notebook or a piece of paper** is great to have on hand in order to keep records. I have included a template in this chapter for you to copy.

5. **Emotional attachment:** Tea leaf reading can be performed with any teacup, but opting to use one you have a history with or a cup that appeals to your aesthetic sensibilities will create a stronger connection.

6. **When deciding on a cup to use, let your intuition guide you.** Hold each one and see how it feels in your hand. Observe what sort of emotional and physical response it elicits.

Choosing a tea

1. **Cut:** Most important, you need to use a loose-leaf tea so the leaves will remain after you've drunk the liquid. It is also important that you choose a high-quality tea. This ensures that there will be more variation in the leaf

size and shape. Bagged tea is not an option. Cutting open a tea bag and pouring the contents into your cup may sound like a good solution, but these leaves are often machine-processed and powdery, so they won't create shapes distinct enough for a reading.

2. **Size:** This is the next most important thing to consider. Leaves that are too small won't be able to build a large enough picture, and leaves that are too big will dominate the cup and obscure any potential messages. Always experiment with size and texture, and remember that when wet, the leaves will expand and unravel a little bit.

3. **Type:** As we learned from my experience with my nana, the type of tea you choose can have a big spiritual impact on your reading. Traditionally, green tea, oolong, and black tea are used, but I encourage you to experiment with different herbal mixtures as well. Always consult a doctor before in-gesting herbs.

You can choose a tea based on the descriptions in the list below, but remember that these are just suggestions. Your own personal associations with the flavors should take precedence.

English breakfast: Black tea

English breakfast has been a staple in homes since the late 1880s. Its origin story varies, but the most supported version of its creation goes like this:

In the late nineteenth century, a Scottish tea master experimented by taking Assam, Ceylon, and Keemun leaves and blending them together. The result was extremely pleasing, and when Queen Victoria was visiting her royal residence in Scotland, she was given a sample of the concoction. Apparently, she loved it so much she brought large stores of it home to England, and the rest is history.

English breakfast is a great choice for all sorts of readings. Anything from career inquiries to relationship troubles are supported by this blend. It also works particularly well for spirit communication, likely due to its overall popularity.

Earl Grey: Black tea

Named for Charles Grey, the second Earl of Grey, this tea is a blend of different black tea leaves. Bergamot oil, which comes from a type of Italian orange tree, is added afterward to give it a stimulating flavor. It is thought that this tea was a gift from a visiting Chinese envoy to the earl.

Similar to English breakfast, Earl Grey works wonderfully for a wide range of readings. This tea is also known for its comforting and calming aroma, which can be beneficial for situations that are emotionally heavy or tense.

Assam: Black tea

Assam is one of the base teas that make up your favorite blends, but it can be used on its own as well. Hailing from the Assam region of India, this tea is bold, earthy, and rich.

Assam is a straightforward and dependable tea and can be suitable for any situation, but its strength and distinct flavor lend themselves well to career and finance readings.

Darjeeling: Black tea

Affectionately known as the champagne of tea, Darjeeling is a fan favorite of many people around the world. This tea varies in strength and profile depending on the time it is harvested, but overall it has a light and fruity taste.

Darjeeling should be reserved for special occasions or sessions due to its reputation and its price tag. It lends itself well to matters of the heart or sensitive situations that require a delicate touch.

Ceylon: Black tea

Ceylon is an incredibly popular tea that is from the high-altitude regions of Sri Lanka. A common base for Earl Grey, this leaf is well-rounded and can carry all sorts of blends, but it works just as well on its own. If you are unsure where to begin working with black tea, Ceylon is a safe and reliable choice.

Ceylon tea plantations reach high in the sky, which can be symbolically interpreted as being closer to heaven. This tea is an obvious choice for spirit communication readings.

Longjing tea a.k.a. Dragon Well tea: Chinese green tea

Dragon Well tea is one of China's most famous teas, and it is beloved by tea connoisseurs around the world. Grown in Zhejiang Province, the leaves are picked only between certain dates, always by hand, and then roasted in a wok, which helps develop the flavor profile.

Due to the ritual of harvesting and the hand preparation of this tea, Dragon Well is an excellent choice for communicating with spirits of all kinds, but especially with those who were craftspeople or considered experts in their trade.

Sencha: Japanese green tea

As the most popular green tea in Japan, sencha is a great choice if you've never tried green tea. It is described as having a bright and fresh taste and is grown under direct sunlight, which is what sets it apart from other green teas.

This sun-soaked tea is great for readings concerning any future goals and/or plans. Use it to get uplifting and inspiring advice about the future.

Oolong: Oolong tea

Oolong tea is neither a black tea nor a green tea and actually falls into a category of its own. When black teas are processed, they are allowed to oxidize fully, whereas green teas barely at all. Oolong is oxidized partially, anywhere from 10 to 80 percent, which can make it sometimes taste like a green tea and at other times like a black tea.

Because this tea is, in a way, "between worlds" due to its processing, it is a natural choice for spirit communication. If you have been struggling to connect with spirits, give oolong a try.

Herbal tea

Herbal teas are a good way to bring plant energy into your session. Herbs can be brewed on their own or mixed with different tea leaves to create blends. I recommend purchasing one of these blends to give more depth to your reading.

If you would like to bring herbs into your séance but don't want to ingest them, try incorporating incense or sprinkling a few leaves around your cup.

Always consult a doctor before working with plants and herbs.

Chamomile: A calming tea, chamomile can help you relax and be more receptive to spirit communication.

Mint: In witchcraft, mint is used for healing and protection and to encourage psychic dreams, which makes it an excellent choice if you perform tasseography before bed.

Ginger: Spicy and warm, ginger is a great herb for readings pertaining to love, relationships, and sex.

Orange: The sweet scent of orange triggers feelings of comfort and nostalgia for many people, so naturally having some dried peels in your tea is great for readings that deal with the past.

Strawberry: Strawberry-flavored black tea is the perfect addition to an afternoon séance. The sweetness of the strawberry is in perfect contrast to the nutty tea leaves. This is a great mixture for all types of readings.

Mugwort: Mugwort has been used for centuries as a protective and spiritual cleansing herb. It is believed to enhance psychic abilities and aid in lucid dreaming. This makes it a wonderful choice to use in tasseography. You don't need much of this herb to reap its benefits, so I recommend mixing it with your favorite green or black tea.

WARNING: Mugwort is an abortifacient and should never be consumed or handled by someone who is pregnant.

TASSEOGRAPHY INSTRUCTIONS

The following method of tasseography can be used for both personal readings and spirit communication.

I do encourage you to find your own style. If something doesn't feel right, it is always best to change it up. Purists may recoil at the notion, but always remember that divination is a very personal journey, and when you're comfortable with your routine, you will be more effective at interpreting messages.

After setting up your séance as outlined in chapter 5 and choosing your tea and cup, follow the steps below.

Instructions

1. Take a teaspoon of your loose-leaf tea and place it in your cup and begin to boil your water. You can experiment with the amount of tea you use, and remember that you won't be adding milk or creamer, so the flavor may be stronger. If multiple people are involved in the session, place the tea directly in a teapot or have each person fill their own cup with leaves.

2. Next, pour the boiled water over the top of the leaves. Be sure to leave approximately a quarter inch of space from the rim.

3. Gently stir your tea while thinking of your question or the situation you are inquiring about.

4. While you are waiting for the tea to be cool enough to drink, you can actually begin divining or interpreting what you see.
   - Lots of bubbles on the surface mean prosperity is heading your way.
   - A stem, leaf, or other "debris" floating on the surface means a visitation is imminent. This can be in reference to a ghostly visitor or a living person.
   - Leaves stuck to the side of the cup also represent visitations. The closer to the handle the leaf is, the sooner the person will arrive. In a spirit reading, leaves near the handle mean a spirit is present.
   - Spilling liquid while stirring foretells that tears will be shed in the near future.

5. When your tea has cooled to a point that you can drink it, begin taking mindful sips. Use your nondominant hand to hold the cup. Your nondominant hand is considered to be your "intuitive hand," and using it is believed to trigger the subconscious. It is strongly advised that you think of your question during this time. Some people even repeat it over and over in their head while drinking.

6. When there is about a teaspoon of liquid left at the bottom of the cup, swirl it three times before flipping it facedown onto the saucer. You do need to do this fairly quickly, so I suggest folding up a piece of paper towel and laying it on the saucer. This not only helps catch the excess liquid and leaves but also provides a safe cushion so you don't break the cup. *This is extra important if you are using a family heirloom.*

7. Next, you will want to either tap three times on the bottom of your over-turned cup or rest your nondominant hand on it for a second or two while thinking of your question. Some people also recommend spinning the cup three times to disperse the leaves.

8. When you feel ready, turn the cup's handle so it is positioned at six o'clock, and flip over the cup and look inside the well. At first glance, you may not see anything other than blobs of tea leaves, but little by little, pictures will begin to form. Don't get discouraged if nothing seems to be appearing. Take your time and look at the contents from different angles. Gently relaxing your eyes or even squinting can help. Though the tea leaves you are supposed to read are in the cup, if it feels natural, you can also take a look at the saucer and see if any images have appeared there.

9. When you start to see images and patterns in the leaves, write them down. You will also want to make note of where in the cup they are located.

10. Now for the fun part: interpreting the images! You can find meanings for the most common images in the dictionary on page 204.

ANATOMY OF THE CUP

The cup is divided into three main parts, each of which holds different meanings for the tea leaves that stick there. None of these are set in stone. Over time, you may even develop your own cup sections and correlations.

Bottom of the cup

In a standard reading, the bottom of the cup represents the distant future. This usually means a few months but can also mean years!

In a spirit reading, the bottom of the cup can represent someone who died a long time ago, most likely twenty years or more.

Middle of the cup

In a standard reading, the middle of the cup, along the sides, represents the near future. Generally, this means a few days to a few weeks.

In a spirit reading, the middle of the cup can represent someone who died six to nineteen years prior.

Top of the cup

In a standard reading, the top of the cup, near the rim, represents the immediate future, most likely within the next twenty-four to forty-eight hours.

In a spirit reading, the top of the cup can represent a recent death, usually within the last five years.

The top of the cup can also represent situations that are very important to you or that could signify a life-changing event.

The handle

The handle of the cup represents our connection to the unconscious mind and the spirit realm. Images located near the handle represent our direct environment, and images across from the handle can represent outside influences.

When working with family spirits, the handle can represent our immediate ancestors, and the farther the leaves are from that point, the further back in your family line the spirit is.

IMAGES

Chances are you will see multiple shapes in the leaves. The biggest one will generally take precedence and set the tone of the reading. The surrounding images then help build the story. However, your gut is always the most important thing in a reading. If something feels more important to you, it probably is.

When reading for another person, ask them what images they see, and share with them which ones you see. They may have special insight or a connection to certain symbols that change their meaning. For example, for me, the appearance of a rose means my grandmother is present, but for someone else it could be the name of the street their father grew up on.

If you don't see anything right away, don't get discouraged. You may find it helpful to photograph your cup and look at it again later.

Images that are crossed, broken, or obscured in some way can indicate troubles or inconsistency.

The clearer the image, the more of an impact it will make on your circumstances.

How you discard the leaves after your reading is up to you. Some people like to just compost them, while others sprinkle them in their garden.

RECORD KEEPING

Date:

Time:

People present:

Tea used:

Séance details (candles, heirlooms, etc.):

Spirits contacted:

Question asked:

Symbols and their location in the cup:

Notes:

TASSEOGRAPHY DICTIONARY

In the cartomancy dictionary, I provided you with both the traditional meanings of the tarot cards and the spirit meanings for each card that I have developed over the years.

For the tasseography dictionary, I have opted to include only the traditional meanings for one hundred of the most popular symbols. There are two important reasons for this.

The first is that there is much more room for personal interpretation when doing a tea leaf reading. I encourage you to develop your own spirit meanings list alongside the traditional meanings while working through this chapter. This list is meant to serve as a jumping-off point for you. Remember that the more work you put into developing your interpretation skills, the more you will get out of your readings.

The second reason is that these symbols have universal meanings that are largely understood by everyone. This allows them to be easily adapted to fit your circumstances. You can also use this dictionary to decipher symbols you encounter using other forms of divination, like scrying.

Acorn: Prosperity is heading your way. Autumn will be a significant time.

Airplane: Long-distance travel. If it is facing toward you, a visitor is coming from far away.

Anchor: Upright: A safe and stable period. Reversed: Being weighed down.

Apple: You possess a great deal of knowledge. Growth and opportunity are arriving.

Arrow: News is traveling quickly. You'll be the target of negativity and gossip.

Axe: You can overcome obstacles with effort.

Baby: A new beginning or the birth of a child.

Balloon: A celebration or party.

Bell: Awakening the dead. A funeral procession is arriving. An announcement.

Birds: Good luck. Traveling in a group.

Boat: A visit from a friend or loved one.

Bone: A spirit visitor. Crossbones represent danger.

Book: Gathering wisdom. Beginning a class or taking up a hobby.

Broom: Clean your surroundings. A change in energy or mindset is needed.

Butterfly: Rebirth and regeneration. A new beginning. A very positive omen.

Candle: Enlightenment. A glimmer of hope. Finding a way.

Cat: A cherished pet. Both good luck and bad luck.

Chain: Being trapped or stuck in circumstances beyond your control.

Circle: The circle of life. Going with the flow.

Clock: Time flies. Feeling overwhelmed or under pressure.

Clouds: A storm is brewing. Trouble is on the way.

Coin: Money is coming. A period of financial stability.

Cross: A warning of impending trouble. Delays and setbacks.

Cup: Joy and celebration. Having all your needs met.

Dagger: A betrayal or being in danger.

Dog: A loyal friend. A cherished pet.

Dots: Success in business. A winning idea. An unexpected windfall.

Duck: Work happening below the surface.

Eagle: Facing a challenge. You will be successful.

Egg: Nurturing a creative endeavor. If broken, you will face disappointment.

Envelope: Unexpected news. Money or bills arriving.

Feather: Spiritual fulfillment. A sign from the heavens. A higher power.

Fire: Prosperity, security, and warmth entering your life.

Fish: The subconscious mind. Focus on your creativity.

Flag: Traveling to another nation. Government or political issues.

Flowers: Eternal love and beauty. A new beginning or a time of growth. A blossoming partnership or romance. Spring will be a significant time.

Goat: Keep your plans secret. Ignore temptation. Avoid gossip.

Grapes: A period of abundance and prosperity.

Gun: A period of distress or discomfort. Being threatened.

Hammer: Overcoming obstacles. Repairing a relationship.

Headstone: An ancestor or deceased loved one is present.

Heart: A happy and secure relationship. A new relationship or moving to the next level. A very positive omen.

Horseshoe: A lucky period. Keep a good luck charm nearby.

Hourglass: Beware of danger. Making an important decision. An enemy masquerades as a friend.

House: Planning for the future. A strong desire for security.

Initials: Represent an important person, place, or thing.

Insect: Pay attention to minor details about a project.

Kettle: An illness. In search of healing. Reconnect with your community.

Key: Living up to your potential. Taking control of a situation.

Kite: Period of growth. Feeling excited about what is to come.

Knife: Quarrels or disputes. Being betrayed. An injury that takes time to heal from.

Ladder: Getting a promotion. Climbing higher on the corporate ladder.

Lamp: Uncovering a hidden secret. Navigating a difficult situation. Exposing the truth.

Letter: Expect important news or bills soon.

Line: Straight: Beginning an important journey. Something or someone life-changing approaches. Wavy: An emotional journey, a period of profound insight. Broken: A journey or relationship is cut short, an ending.

Lion: Be courageous now. Take pride in your accomplishments. An influential friend will help you.

Lock: Proceed with caution. Obstacles block your way.

Log: Hard work yields great rewards.

Moon: Spirits roam. Being divinely guided toward success.

Mountain: Being surrounded by powerful people. Accomplishing something great with lots of hard work.

Mouse: Falling prey to a thief or criminal. Betrayal by a friend.

Mushroom: Becoming a leader. Fighting for the respect you deserve.

Necklace: Something precious. Having lots of admirers or suitors.

Numbers: Days, months, weeks. A birthday or anniversary. A house number.

Owl: Seeking wisdom. The gift of second sight. Developing psychic abilities.

Palm tree: Material acquisition. Receiving an inheritance. Summer will be a significant time.

Parrot: Suffering from imposter syndrome. Someone taking credit for your work.

Pine tree: A family gathering. Winter will be a significant time.

Question mark: Searching for answers you aren't meant to know. Ask again later.

Rabbit: Fertility and growth. Working hard on a project. Feeling shy or nervous.

Rainbow: The spirit of a pet is present. All your wishes will come true.

Rake: Tie up loose ends. Create space for new things to flourish.

Raven: The gift of prophecy or healing. A warning about a loss or sickness.

Ring: A romantic engagement. An offer you can't refuse.

Rose: A symbol of good luck. Everlasting love. Take time to appreciate what you have.

Scales: Facing legal issues. Balance and harmony will be restored.

Scissors: Breaking free from a toxic situation. A separation is imminent.

Shark: Hidden danger. An enemy lurks among friends. Feelings of anxiety and worry.

Shell: A spiritual offering. Being protected by your ancestors.

Ship: Beginning a long journey. A significant period of time.

Shoe: Being on the correct path. Return to simplicity. Adapting to changes.

Sickle: Holding on to anger or pain. Lack of self-control or willpower. A long illness or grieving period.

Skull: A warning of danger. Power struggles or disputes.

Snake: Someone untrustworthy. Small misfortunes and setbacks.

Spider: Being recognized for your efforts. Receiving rewards. A time to create.

Squirrel: Preparing for the future. Being blessed in love and friendship.

Stairs: Spirit communication. Looking at a situation from a new angle. Family matters or situations relating to the home.

Star: A very positive omen. An important victory. Keep hope alive.

Sun: Finding peace of mind in relation to a difficult situation. Good times ahead.

Table: A period of stability. Feeling grounded and supported.

Teardrops: Being in mourning. Tears will be shed soon.

T.R. Oldfield & Co., Ltd.

Loose Leaf Spirit Tea.

A Large and Well-Assorted Range

No. 03

No. 07

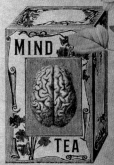

No. 13

More Products Available!

Cups And Saucers.
Tea Pots.

Spoons.
And Much More!

Tower: A new beginning. A new job.

Triangle: Good luck. Fortunate events or meetings.

Turtle: Dedication and persistence. Take your time. Be cautious in your actions.

Umbrella: Protection from harm. Loved ones are watching over you.

Volcano: Emotions are reaching their boiling point. Settle disputes quickly.

Wasp: A negative omen. A serious warning. Betrayal by a loved one.

Wheel: Keep moving forward. Adopt a positive attitude.

Wolf: Loyalty to family and friends. Finding your place in the world.

Zebra: A new opportunity. A change in direction.

DICTIONARY EXERCISE

Write your own meanings for the following symbols:

Anvil:

_____

_____

Bed:

_____

_____

Bumblebee:

_____

_____

Claw:

_____

_____

Daisy:

_____

_____

Ear:

_____

Fox:

_____

_____

Nail:

_____

_____

Trident:

_____

_____

Worm:

_____

_____

Learning to interpret the symbols and then tell the story can be tricky, especially if you are a beginner, but don't give up. Remember: Your first impression is generally correct. Sometimes a reading is meant to help develop your technique instead of providing you with a message.

Sample reading 1
Knife, heart, and anchor
You were betrayed by your partner, and though this action was painful, when your heart heals you will discover that they freed you from being weighed down by the relationship.

Sample reading 2
Lamp, fish, and clock
You are searching for answers that you already have. Listen to your intuition and you will know what to do when the time is right.

Notice how in both of these readings, it is about taking the meaning of the symbol and applying it to a situation in order to tell a story.

11

Rhabdomancy

WHAT IS RHABDOMANCY?

Rhabdomancy is the act of divining or dowsing by using special sticks or rods known as divining rods or dowsing rods. Rhabdomancy can also be performed with a tool known as a pendulum.

Dowsing is a centuries-old practice of divining the locations of things that are hidden underground, such as water, gemstones, and even graves.

Rhabdomancy, like all methods of divination, can also be used to communicate with spirits, which is what I will be teaching you in this chapter.

Before we begin, we must have a clear understanding of the tools you will be using.

While dowsing rods and divining rods pretty much mean the same thing today, they do have historical differences that need to be explained.

A **dowsing rod** is a forked tree branch that is in the shape of a Y and usually between one and two feet long. These special sticks are either found on the ground or deliberately cut from a tree. They are most commonly used for mineral hunting and water divining (also known as water witching), but in the United States some people search for petroleum instead of water, which is called doodlebugging.

A dowsing rod is used by holding one of the forks of the stick (the top of the Y) in each hand while the length (the bottom of the Y) is sticking out straight in front of you. The branch should be parallel to the ground. When the branch signals that it has found something, it either tugs downward or pulls upward.

Divining rods are two L-shaped metal rods that are each about a foot and a half in length. These rods can be used for not only dowsing but also asking specific yes or no questions.

They are generally used in place of the old branch dowsing rods these days.

A rod is held in each hand by the shorter side of the L. The lengths are then held straight ahead of the body, parallel to the ground. When an object is located or a question is answered, the rods either cross over each other or push apart.

A **pendulum** is a weighted object, such as a gemstone or precious metal, that hangs suspended from a chain or thin cord. The other end of the chain is held in one hand, and when a question is answered, the weight moves.

It is essential to understand that no matter which tool is being used, the hands are kept completely still, and in theory, they are then moved by a spirit. This means that rhabdomancy is a form of channeling.

Despite being considered a pseudoscientific practice, dowsing is still used by a wide range of people. I have even heard stories of plumbers who employ the rods in order to find hidden leaks!

A BRIEF HISTORY OF DOWSING

Modern dowsing came into fashion during the sixteenth century in Germany and quickly spread through Western Europe. Its original purpose was to locate gemstones and other precious metals tucked away in underground mines.

By the end of the seventeenth century, people were using dowsing rods to locate water, buried treasure, and, in some cases, even dead bodies.

One of these gruesome body discoveries came up time and time again during my research for this chapter. It is the story of a famous dowser named Jacques Aymar.

In the late 1600s, a Dauphiné man named Jacques was out water witching, which was something he often did with moderate success. On this particular day, however, he was feeling lucky. He roamed the woods on the outskirts of town, his dowsing rod thrust out in front of him.

As he made his way through the grass and fallen leaves, his trusty branch violently jerked to the left. Jacques was ecstatic as he had never felt such a strong pull before. This must've been a very large spring indeed.

But when Jacques began to dig in the location indicated by the rod, he was horrified to see not water but the decomposing corpse of a woman from the village who had been missing for several months.

Jacques brought word of his discovery back to the town and even took it upon himself to find out who had hurt the poor woman. As the dowsing rod had shown the location where she had lain, Jacques decided it would also reveal the murderer.

He pointed the branch at the citizens one by one, and one by one they were found to be innocent. When Jacques reached the widower of the dead woman, however, the branch jerked violently once again.

The horrified former husband of the woman fled immediately, affirming his guilt in the eyes of the townspeople, and Jacques became a local hero.

There are more stories of Jacques solving crimes with his dowsing rod, including a robbery that propelled him to national fame, but I wonder: did the ghost of the dead woman actually direct Jacques to her body and her killer, or did he stumble upon it coincidentally, and this discovery just happened to spook the husband into fleeing?

PERFORMING A SÉANCE WITH DIVINING RODS

As I mentioned at the beginning of this chapter, divining rods can be used to locate objects or for communicating with spirits. I will be walking you through the steps for using them in a séance, but I have also included exercises to help you bond with your tools. The exercises can be performed with both divining rods and pendulums.

Choosing your rods

Deciding on a set of divining rods to purchase is a very simple process, as they generally come in only one size and have just small variations in weight. While they can come in an array of metals, copper is the most common. Copper is a highly conductive metal that's thought to be especially sensitive to spirit activity. If you feel called to experiment with different types, use the metal correspondences on pages 241–42 of the charm casting section.

> TIP: If you can't afford to purchase a set of divining rods, you can make your own by cutting two metal coat hangers, bending them into the correct shape, and then fitting plastic straws to the ends to act as handles. There are many great tutorials available online that cover this in greater depth.

Instructions

1. Open your séance by following the steps in chapter 5. Be sure to have a list of questions prepared. They should be in a yes or no format and not overly complicated. You may find it helpful to record your session so you don't need to pause to write down the answers you receive.

2. Hold one rod loosely in each hand in front of you while you focus on the spirit you would like to communicate with. The rods should be in the neutral position (which is directly ahead of you, parallel to each other and the

ground). You may find standing to be more comfortable, but if your arms get tired, you can sit and rest your elbows on a table.

3. This next step is very important, and you should spend a few minutes here. Begin by asking the spirit to confirm what a "yes" and a "no" look like with the rods. In most cases, the "yes" is when the rods cross over each other, and a "no" is when they push away from each other. Ask the spirit to confirm each action multiple times, allowing the rods to return to the neutral position in between.

   - After you are confident in each movement, you will confirm that the person you are speaking with is the one you *want* to be speaking with.

     For example, ask out loud, "Is my grandfather Charles in the room?" If the rods indicate yes, proceed to the next question or step in the séance. If they indicate no, close the séance.

   - Now you may be thinking that a spirit could just answer yes in order to communicate with someone. This is where your personal boundaries will come into play.

     Listen to your intuition. Do you feel confident that it is indeed your grandfather Charles? Or do you need to ask a few more follow-up questions? Try to tailor the questions to reflect things that only he would know.

   - Again, if anything feels uncomfortable or negative, end the séance.

4. When you are satisfied with the answers, thank the spirit for their patience and cooperation and let them know you are ready to continue on with the rest of your questions.

5. Begin asking each question out loud. Remember to pause briefly for a response. If no answer comes, you can repeat the question once more. If you still don't receive an answer after that, move on to the next question.

6. When all questions are asked and the spirits are thanked, you can end the séance.

PERFORMING A SÉANCE WITH A PENDULUM

The steps for using a pendulum are exactly the same as they are for the divining rods. The only difference is that you are holding the pendulum with one hand straight out in front of you (remember to use your nondominant hand). "Yes" and "no" will be determined by different movements, such as swings and circles, which are controlled by the spirit.

Choosing a pendulum

You can add special energetic layers to your séance by choosing your pendulum based on the metaphysical properties of the weight.

Metal: An all-metal pendulum is a great choice when beginning your practice. Use the suggestions on pages 241–42 in the charm casting section to help you pick an appropriate one.

Gemstone: Most pendulums available on the market are made with polished gemstone points attached to metal chains.

Amethyst: This crystal is part of the quartz family and is thought to open the third eye and enhance psychic abilities.

Rainbow moonstone: A manifesting stone, this is an excellent choice for calling on spirits to help you with difficult situations or big life events.

Rose quartz: This crystal of love is, of course, best used for matters relating to the heart, but it can also help boost your confidence.

Black tourmaline: This gemstone is often used to absorb negative energy. If your séance is related to grief and mourning, this stone makes a good ally.

Angelite: If you are hoping to communicate with a spirit guide or perhaps a guardian angel, use this stone, as it dispels fears and doubts.

Citrine: The mind-clearing properties of citrine can be harnessed when you need help focusing on a specific spirit or situation.

SILVER PENDULUMS

ARCHER DIVINATION TOOLS

No. 113.

No. 110.

No. 116.

No. 112.

No. 114.

Points in favor of Archer Silver Pendulums

Equal to gold in finish and good looks. The finest silver finishes ensure your
will last for years and years.

onlt to give these Archer Pendulums a trial to be convinced of their
ty.

ARCHER DIVINATION TOOLS

Sodalite: Sodalite helps to develop intuition and also removes negative feelings and confusion often associated with spirit communication.

Clear quartz: Grounding, protective, and cleansing, this crystal can come in handy when inquiring about a broad range of topics and situations.

Lapis lazuli: This is a popular choice when speaking with spirits, as this stone encourages communication and understanding.

RHABDOMANCY EXERCISES

Dowsing may seem simple, but it actually takes a lot of practice to do correctly. You will want to consistently work on it by practicing various exercises with your tools.

Exercise 01

1. Gather a large quantity of one item, such as jelly beans.

2. Take a handful and place them on the table in front of you (you should not count them).

3. Take your divining rods or pendulum and hold them over the jelly beans.

4. Confirm the movements for "yes" and "no."

5. Ask the following questions. Substitute your own numbers.

   - Are there more than ten jelly beans? Yes.
   - Are there more than twenty jelly beans? Yes.
   - Are there more than thirty jelly beans? No.
   - Are there more than twenty-five jelly beans? No.
   - Are there twenty-one jelly beans? No.
   - Are there twenty-two jelly beans? No.
   - Are there twenty-three jelly beans? Yes.

- Are there twenty-four jelly beans? No. (Always go one number above and below to confirm.)
- Are there twenty-three jelly beans? Yes.

According to the rods, twenty-three jelly beans is the final answer. At this point you will count them and see how close you were. If you were off by a large margin, try doing this exercise more often. The last step, of course, is to eat the jelly beans.

Exercise 02

This exercise can be performed if you are interested in the treasure hunting, or traditional, form of dowsing.

Gather some of the following items: jewelry, precious metals such as gold and silver, a cup of water, a dish of soil, and various types of wood.

1. Begin by confirming your movements for "yes" and "no." Do this multiple times.

2. Next, place each object one by one on a table and hold the rods or pendulum above them. I will be using a gold ring as the example.

With your rods above the ring, ask the question "Is this a gold ring?" If yes, confirm this one time before moving on to the next object. If the answer is no, try asking again or switching out the object and trying again.

Make note of which objects the rods identified correctly and for which objects the answers were wrong or inconclusive.

RECORD KEEPING

Date:

Time:

People present:

Tool used:

Séance details (candles, heirlooms, etc.):

Spirits contacted:

Question asked:

Notes:

12

A Scientific Séance

EVPs, SPIRIT PHOTOGRAPHY, AND MODERN TOOLS

The idea that science and the paranormal have always been at odds is actually a relatively new concept. During the nineteenth and twentieth centuries, the two went hand in hand. The world's most brilliant minds were actively engaged in all areas of spiritualism.

For as long as we have been recording sounds and capturing images, we have been using this technology to speak to and prove the existence of ghosts.

Ghostly messages have come across radio waves, telephone lines, and television stations—some as clear as day, others just a faint shadow or distorted whisper.

WHAT IS EVP?

Electronic voice phenomena, or EVP for short, are recordings that contain spirit voices. There can be no other plausible explanation for their existence, not even environmental or electronic interference.

What is this phenomenon and how did it start? And more importantly, how can you use this modern technology to enhance your séance?

The devices used to capture these voices include tape recorders, digital recorders, reel-to-reels, and all other equipment capable of recording sound.

EVPs have captured voices and sounds that are thought to have come from both **residual hauntings** and **intelligent hauntings**.

These recordings contain voices that range in terms of gender, age, and spoken language and are ranked in quality using certain criteria.

Good: Clear and distinct messages. Can be heard without any adjustment to volume or manipulation of the audio. These recordings often contain full sentences.

Moderate: Moderately clear messages. These recordings may be heard only with volume adjustments, and only some words may be comprehensible.

Poor: Unclear or extremely quiet messages. To be heard, these recordings require sound-filtering software or other enhancements. The recordings are often inconclusive, and the audibility issues are considered to be the result of environmental factors or electronic interference.

History of early spirit technology

Ghost phones

I have been at work for some time building an apparatus to see if it is possible for personalities which have left this earth to communicate

with us . . . If this is ever accomplished it will be accomplished not by any occult, mystifying, mysterious or weird means, such as are employed by so-called mediums, but by scientific methods.
—Thomas Edison for *The American Magazine*, 1920

It is believed that before his death in 1931, the famous inventor Thomas Edison was hard at work on a device that he hoped could be used to speak with spirits.

Edison spent his life modifying inventions in order to make them more efficient. Given that he was a spiritualist, creating a device capable of recording spirit voices was the height of efficiency. To Edison, his "spirit phone" would make the world better because it would make séances easier. If he had succeeded, spirit messages might be as common as all other aspects of our daily life, no more unusual than receiving a phone call or sending an email.

Many people dispute the existence of this machine, as no plans or prototypes have ever been found. But given how involved Edison was in the paranormal community, it is a safe bet that this machine was more than just hearsay.

The inventor . . . looks upon the world and is not contented with things as they are. He wants to improve whatever he sees, he wants to benefit the world; he is haunted by an idea. The spirit of invention possesses him, seeking materialization.
—Alexander Graham Bell

In 1876, the Scottish inventor Alexander Graham Bell created his most famous invention: the telephone.

He was only twenty-nine years old when he was awarded the patent, and by his thirtieth birthday, news surrounding the telephone had taken the world by storm.

However, to understand how this invention came to be, we need to once again look at spiritualism.

Alexander and his brother Edward were avid believers in the movement, and even made a macabre promise to each other. The first one of the pair who died would send a message to the other from the great beyond.

Tragically, Edward died in 1867, at just nineteen years old, and Alexander, not one to wait around, began working on a device to contact the dead with the help of his assistant, who also happened to be a medium.

The telephone was likely born out of a combination of intelligence and grief. It provided people with the ability to contact the ones they loved most.

To this day, many people still claim to have received phone calls from spirits, and there are mediums who work exclusively with the telephone as a conduit.

Most common beliefs about EVPs

They are the result of pareidolia.
Audio pareidolia is the act of misinterpreting random noises into patterns that your brain can recognize. One famous example is satanic backmasking, which is the belief that musicians record satanic messages backward into their songs to brainwash their listeners.

They are a hoax.
Many skeptics believe that EVPs are prerecorded by paranormal investigators in order to boost ratings on television or secure more jobs.

They are the result of interference.
This is actually the case with many EVPs. Conversations or outside noises are often inadvertently recorded. I will be providing you with tips to make sure you don't accidentally give yourself a false EVP.

The most famous EVPs

Konstantin Raudive collection
Latvian writer and parapsychologist Konstantin Raudive created one of the most extensive collections of EVPs ever, totaling somewhere between seventy thousand and a hundred thousand recordings.

He believed that the messages he received were from influential people such

SPIRIT PHOTOGRAPHY CAMERAS

BURBANK PHOTO COMPANY

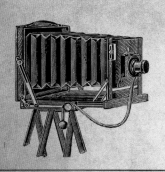

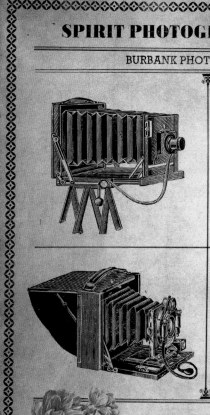

T...ONES NOW AVAILABLE

Try you... ...d at the newest phenomenon in spirit
communi...ation! **TELEPHONE DIVINATION!**
W... h... ...best selection of telephone equipment.

...an... ...OICES and **MESSAGES** from the great
...nd in the comfort of your own home.

...edium required.

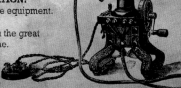

as politicians and artists. The languages spoken in these EVPs were predominantly German, Latvian, and French.

How to perform a séance using EVP

1. Gather your tools and open your séance using the guide in chapter 5.

2. Turn on your recorder and state out loud the date, time, who is physically present with you, and whom you are attempting to contact.

3. Begin by inviting the chosen spirit into the space with you. Explain what you are doing and why you would like to communicate.

4. Next, you can start asking questions. Be sure to leave sufficient space for a response after each question. Remember that unless you are capable of listening in real time, you will most likely learn if you received a response only after the séance is finished and you play back the recording.

5. When finished, thank the spirit for their time and close the séance.

6. Upload the file to your computer and play it back.

7. Did you receive any responses?

Tips
Everyone present should always speak loudly and clearly. Too often, when people in the room whisper, these sounds are misinterpreted as EVPs.

Make note of any fans, heaters, construction noise, house sounds, or loud neighbors before you begin.

Turn off all your electronics and put your phone on "Do not disturb."

SPIRIT PHOTOGRAPHY

What is spirit photography?

For as long as there have been cameras, there have been spirit photographs.

Spirit photography is the act of intentionally or unintentionally capturing a ghost in a photograph.

Spirit photography can likely be credited as the precursor to the abundance of ghost-hunting television shows and podcasts that many of us enjoy today. Everyone wants to see a ghost for themselves, even if they aren't necessarily believers in the paranormal.

Spirit photography history

In the mid- to late 1800s, photography was a rapidly expanding art form. New techniques were being created constantly, and when paired with spiritualist beliefs, this new technology led to a lucrative market known as spirit photography.

The first widely recognized spirit photographer was a man named William Mumler, who worked in Boston and New York. Mumler claimed to have actually fallen into the profession by accident.

One day, after taking a self-portrait, Mumler realized that the photo showed not only himself but the ghostly image of his deceased cousin as well.

Spiritualism was a common interest Mumler shared with his wife, Hannah, who was herself a medium and a spiritual healer. It is safe to believe that she played a pivotal role in the creation of the business, as she would have had many clients interested in having a spirit portrait taken.

The couple successfully managed the business for a number of years, selling countless photographs...that is, until the accusations of fraud began to roll in.

America was actively engaged in the Civil War at this time, a war in which thousands of people died every day. Surviving family members and loved ones were still actively grieving, and critics believed that the Mumlers were preying on that grief.

Today when we think of photo manipulation, we generally think of Photoshop. This powerful software can be used to alter anything on a screen, but photo manipulation has actually been around a lot longer.

Civil War–era photographers were able to partially expose film and mess with photos during the development process, and so spirit images were widely faked.

Because of this, accusations mounted against the now-famous Mumler, and in 1869, he could evade them no longer. He was arrested on fraud charges, and a trial by judge soon followed.

Mumler was eventually acquitted because the prosecutor ultimately could not prove guilt beyond a reasonable doubt. But Mumler's reputation and business never fully recovered, and he died in poverty.

Despite the downfall of the father of spirit photography, the practice continued well into the twentieth century.

The most famous spirit photograph

Ghost of Abraham Lincoln by William Mumler, circa 1869

The most famous of Mumler's photos shows a seated Mary Todd Lincoln, avid spiritualist and wife of President Abraham Lincoln. Behind her there is a faint outline of her husband resting his hands on her shoulders.

Supposedly, the widow used a pseudonym during the session, though it is doubtful that William Mumler didn't know who she was.

How to use spirit photography to enhance your séance

While you can't use photography in order to actively communicate with a spirit in a divinatory sense, you can use it alongside your séance.

Video: Set up a video camera to record while you are in session. Be sure to have your entire workspace in the frame. You don't need to purchase any fancy equipment: your phone and a tripod will work just fine. If you want to take it a step further, you can use a thermal camera.

Photo: Set up your camera to snap photos while you are in a session. Be sure to have your entire workspace in the frame. On most digital cameras you can set up a timer, but it is much easier to have a remote trigger that you can press manually. There are many remote triggers available now that work with digital cameras or your phone's built-in camera.

WARNING: Too often people believe they have captured a spirit in the form of an "orb," which looks like a glowing white ball. Really, they have just captured particles such as dust, light reflections, or insects.

PARANORMAL INVESTIGATORS' TOOL KIT

Like the spiritualists, modern-day paranormal investigators are constantly working with new technologies. Below is a list of suggestions for your kit.

EVP recorder: This is a small recorder that has a built-in microphone and speaker. Most have a headphone jack, so you can listen in real time.

Ghost box or spirit box: This device uses radio wave sweeps, which means it changes its frequency quickly to produce white noise and static that spirits can manipulate in order to convey messages. These tools play back in real time but are also capable of recording.

EMF meter: This tool detects changes in electromagnetic energy. These spikes are thought to be the result of ghostly energy.

Digital camera and video camera: Cameras are often used to capture images that can't be seen by the naked eye, or to gather evidence of interactions, such as objects moving when nobody is physically present to witness them.

Thermometer and thermal imaging camera: These tools are used to measure changes in temperature as spirits are thought to produce "cold spots," which are chilly areas that can't be explained by their environment.

Flashlight: Since most investigations are done at night, this is always a useful tool to keep on hand.

Batteries: It is thought that spirits manipulate energy around them in order to communicate; therefore, keeping spare batteries around for your equipment is always a good idea.

13

More Types of Casting Divination

In this chapter, I am providing you with instructions for two very different forms of casting divination. The tradition of casting lots, also known
as sortilege, has been practiced by almost every culture. Items used in
casting divination can be eclectic in nature, or they can be structured and
part of a matching set.

WHAT IS CHARM CASTING/CHARM DIVINATION?

Most people enjoy jewelry and have at least one item that is precious to
them, such as a wedding band or a family heirloom. These items are symbolic of love and happiness, feelings we cherish.

Curated sets of jewelry charms, like the ones found on charm bracelets, can also be used in divination, and are a wonderful way to add more
messages and layers to your readings. You can use a broad range of

charms together as a set, or you can create smaller sets designed for specific readings. For instance, a love reading set could contain charms like hearts, birds, flowers, and initials.

Charm casting is very affordable, which makes it a great option if you want to try something new without breaking the bank. You can build a well-functioning set of fifteen to twenty charms for under ten dollars.

Because you can personalize your charms to suit your taste, you may also want to consider incorporating different colors or metals into your set in order to enhance your readings.

A brief history of charm bracelets, from magical to decorative and back again

Humans have been carrying charms for almost as long as we have existed.

Sacred items made of bone, wood, shell, and stone acted as both amulets (magical items worn for protection) and talismans (magical items worn to attract something, such as good luck).

The oldest jewelry found to date was discovered in a cave in the southern region of South Africa, and is roughly seventy-five thousand years old! These beads, which archaeologists believe were worn on bracelets or necklaces, pre-date jewelry found in Europe by roughly thirty thousand years.

One thing that makes these beads so special is that they were coated with a red ocher pigment that was also used to decorate tools and stones found in the same area. This lends credence to the belief that the beads represented some type of importance or social standing.

In Ancient Egypt, charms were items that were both practical and decorative. Fashioned from metal and precious stones, they imbued the wearer with power and protection, regardless of whether the person was living or dead.

During the Victorian era in Britain, charm bracelets became all the rage due to Queen Victoria's embracing the jewelry style. Everything the queen did or said her subjects soon copied.

As a woman who took death and mourning incredibly seriously, Queen Victoria had a special charm bracelet made to honor her late husband, Albert. It included a miniature photo of him alongside a locket containing some of his hair.

In the first half of the twentieth century, charm bracelets were a practical jewelry item to own, especially if you didn't have much disposable income, a reality for many due to multiple wars that took place and, in America, the Great Depression. If another item of jewelry you owned broke and you couldn't afford to fix it, it could find a new purpose on your bracelet.

Charm bracelets have long been a staple in our world and have never gone out of fashion. This makes using charms in divination a wonderful way to connect with not only your own spirit but the spirits of all other humans who have loved and used charms throughout history.

Energetic properties of metals

Copper

A conductive metal, copper is thought to increase psychic abilities and intuition. Copper stimulates and energizes the mind while working to clear our negative energy. Copper is a practical metal, which makes it suitable for seeking advice about your day-to-day circumstances.

Brass

Brass is an alloy, which means it is made up of more than one metal, in this case copper and zinc. Not only does it increase psychic abilities; it is also believed to increase courage and focus.

Pewter

Pewter is a metal made by combining large amounts of tin with small amounts of copper or bismuth. Until recently, pewter contained lead, so you should exercise caution when interacting with it. Energetically speaking, pewter increases luck and encourages finding your personal power and hidden talents.

Stainless steel

Stainless steel is a powerhouse in today's world. It is an alloy of iron and chromium, and it's corrosion-resistant, which makes it a great choice for a long-lasting charm set. Iron has long been believed to protect against malevolent ghosts and spirits, which makes stainless steel an excellent go-to for divination beginners.

Gold

Gold is the most valuable and sought-after metal there is. Wars have been waged over it, and people have died alone in the wilderness searching for it. Gold represents universal knowledge and spiritual understanding. Having a charm set entirely made of gold would be expensive, so I recommend choosing one gold charm that represents you and mixing it into the rest of your set.

Silver

Silver is another precious metal that has great cultural significance for humans. Because silver is highly reflective and resistant to high temperatures, its value comes from both beauty and practicality. Silver promotes spiritual balance and inner peace and also increases your intuition.

Some people mix other items into their sets, such as bones, coins, teeth, shells, and gemstones. Don't be afraid to experiment and try different combinations. You can find gemstone properties on page 219 in the chapter on pendulums and dowsing (chapter 11, "Rhabdomancy").

How to cast charms

There are two ways that I cast charms, and both are equally valuable.

The first is to randomly pull one or two charms from their storage container (such as a bowl or bag) without looking and use them to enhance a reading you've already performed with another divination method, such as cartomancy or tasseography.

In this scenario, the charms are used to confirm messages or explain confusing parts of a reading. This is perfect if you are a beginner and working on becoming more confident in your practice.

If you would like to go deeper with your charm reading, then follow the instructions on the next page.

1. Gather all your charms and place them in a bowl large enough to move your hand around in freely. Next, take a blank piece of paper and create four equal sections by drawing a line through the center vertically and then horizontally.

2. At the top of each section, write the following headers:

   - **Top left section:** Write "Fire," which represents creative and spiritual matters.
   - **Top right section:** Write "Earth," which represents health and financial matters.
   - **Bottom left section:** Write "Water," which represents emotional and relationship matters.
   - **Bottom right section:** Write "Air," which represents intellectual and psychological matters.

3. When you are ready, open your séance using the steps outlined in chapter 5.

4. Think of your question, or the spirit with which you wish to communicate, while you mix the charms in the bowl with your nondominant hand. Do not look at the charms or try to feel for specific ones. Just focus on your question.

5. When you're ready, grab a small handful of charms. Then hold your fist a few inches above the center of the paper with the four sections.

6. Say your question one final time, either out loud or in your head, as you open your hand above the paper. The charms will now fall in their respective sections to be interpreted. Charms that have fallen outside the paper perimeter can be disregarded unless you feel an intuitive pull to include them.

7. When you are finished with your reading, be sure to thank the spirits and close your séance.

RECORD KEEPING

Date:

Time:

People present:

Charm metal:

Séance details (candles, heirlooms, etc.):

Spirits contacted:

Question asked:

Charms received:

Notes:

✳ FINE SOLID 10k. GOLD CHARMS. ✳

These Charms are all Full Figures, and are not Flat and Engraved.
Good Styles.   Good Quality.   Good Finish.

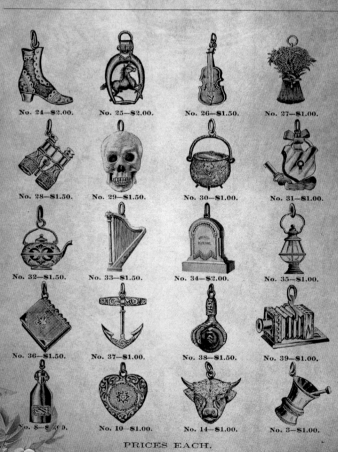

No. 24—$2.00.	No. 25—$2.00.	No. 26—$1.50.	No. 27—$1.00.
No. 28—$1.50.	No. 29—$1.50.	No. 30—$1.00.	No. 31—$1.00.
No. 32—$1.50.	No. 33—$1.50.	No. 34—$2.00.	No. 35—$1.00.
No. 36—$1.50.	No. 37—$1.00.	No. 38—$1.50.	No. 39—$1.00.
No. 8—$ .00.	No. 10—$1.00.	No. 14—$1.00.	No. 3—$1.00.

PRICES EACH.

CHARM DICTIONARY

The following dictionary will provide you with the meanings for the charms I have in my personal set. Be sure to write your own definitions as well, because the more you can personalize your charms the better!

Planets:

Sun: Sunday, the daytime, joy, happiness

Moon: Monday, the nighttime, secrets, mysteries

Mercury: Wednesday, communication, intellect

Venus: Friday, love, beauty

Mars: Tuesday, war and destruction, anger

Jupiter: Thursday, luck, expansion

Saturn: Saturday, restriction, karma

Uranus: Rebellion and chaos, trying new things

Neptune: Disillusionment, dreaming of spirit, intuition

Pluto: The underworld, where spirits roam, death and taxes

Zodiac:

Represents the twelve zodiac signs: Aries, Taurus, Gemini, Cancer, Leo, Virgo, Libra, Scorpio, Sagittarius, Capricorn, Aquarius, and Pisces

Letters:

Represent people's names, places

Numbers:

Represent dates and anniversaries, addresses

Food and drink:

Teacup: Perform tasseography, need for healing, relaxation

Coffee: Wake up, need for stimulation, creativity

Teapot: Gossip or sensitive information, community issues

Potion: Transformation and change, taking a chance

Cup: A vessel, half-full or half-empty, prosperity

Spoon: Satisfaction, matters of the home, wealth or inheritance

Grapes: Fertility and abundance, wealth, materialism, luxury

Apple: Gift of knowledge, question the status quo, good health

Pumpkin: The mysterious realm, in-between worlds, change

Cupcake: Sweetness, good times and celebration, happiness

Wheat: Fertility of Mother Earth, abundance, growth

Corn: Longevity, protection, abundance and sustenance

Nature:

Flower: Friendship, joy, beauty, eternal life

Rose: Purity and innocence, everlasting love, a new relationship

Lightning: Illumination, destruction of old beliefs, sudden insight

Shooting star: A wish coming true

Star: A guiding light, hope for the future

Clover: A symbol of good luck, protection from harm

Snowflake: Being unique, fragility of life, cold and aloof

Tree: New life, evolution, change, wisdom and power

Shell: Fertility, good fortune

Feather: A gift from the divine, soaring above the competition

Animals:

Bee: Hard work and organization, mastering a trade

Owl: Seeking wisdom and clarity, giving or receiving advice

Raven: A messenger from the underworld, spiritual insight

Bat: Guardian of the underworld, soul journey, rebirth

Turtle: Perseverance, protecting oneself

Cat: Mystery and cunning, in the shadows

Dragonfly: Magic in the ordinary, growth and maturity

Elephant: Protection, remove obstacles, strength

Hare: Rebirth and resurrection, fertility, make haste

Lion: Reclaiming your power, becoming a leader

Tiger: The hunter, fearlessness, bravery

Zebra: Individualism, don't be afraid to stand out
Frog: Personal transformation, between worlds
Wolf: Loyalty and family, finding community
Dinosaur: The past, karma, unearthing secrets
Pig: Good fortune, humor and silliness
Monkey: Entertainment, playfulness, agility, resourcefulness
Horse: Desire for freedom, a companion, courage
Bear: A period of solitude, primal instincts
Deer: Return to nature, grace, peace
Starfish: Becoming more self-sustainable, adaptability
Spider: Weaving fate, creation, the details

Human:

People: Represents people in your life or maturity levels
Skeleton: Being haunted, spirit visitor, the past
Zombie: Can't let go, feeling afraid, forcing something
Skull and crossbones: Warning, a dangerous threat, poison

Mythical:

Magic lantern: Make a wish, changing circumstances
Fairy: Magical moments, illusions, tricks, imagination
Dragon: Royalty or a position of power, tall tales
Pentacle: The elements, natural forces, protection
Goddess and god figures: The divine, a deity, have faith
Spiral: Ancient power and knowledge, realm of the dead

Objects:

Nesting doll: Look within, intuition
Sword: Chivalry, power, protection, following tradition
Knife: Bickering and fighting, betrayal
Axe: Removing obstacles, clearing a path
Scissors: Turning one thing into two, crafting your destiny, removing toxic influences

Shovel: Digging up the past, burying the past, gravedigging

Wrench: Repairing something, relieving pressure

Broom: Cleanse (physically or energetically), remove negativity

Gavel: Legal issues, justice, power

Key: Having control, freedom, hiding something

Umbrella: Protection, hiding, safe from a bad influence

Signpost: Look for a sign, you know what to do

Playing cards: Luck, perform cartomancy

Book: Looking for answers, a period of study, advancing in career

Compass: Feeling lost, searching for something, change direction

Boat: A spiritual journey, unknown territory

Anchor: Feeling secure, period of stability

Airplane: A physical journey, visitors

Shoes: Stay grounded, short travels, head into the shadows

Purse: Resources, magical ingredients

Money: Financial security, monetary wealth, inheritance, generational wealth or poverty

Crown: High status, royalty, business success, climbing the corporate ladder

Armor: Nobility, doing what is right, protecting yourself

Magic wand: Power from within, creation, changing fate

Musical note: Tradition, a special gift, bringing community together

Clock: Time, past/present/future, daily life

Hat: Connection to the spirit world, modesty, authority

Fan: Sophistication and wealth, inspiration

DOMINO DIVINATION

What is domino divination?

The second form of divination in this chapter is the art of casting dominoes.

Reading dominoes is a fun and convenient divinatory method worth trying.

PREMIUM DOMINOES

CASTING TOOLS

❧

JUST $5.00 PER SET.

KEEPSAKE BOX IN OAK FINISH. AUTHENTIC BONE TILES.

❧

POPOVICH & CO.,

CASTING TOOLS

Chances are you already have a set lying around your home just waiting to be utilized in this new way.

Dominoes are small white rectangular tiles that come in a set of twenty-eight. Though these days dominoes are made of plastic, they were originally made from bone or ivory.

The black dots on each tile represent the faces of two dice. Western dominoes are unique in that sets also contain certain tiles that depict only one die face on one side and a blank face on the other. There is also one tile in the game that is completely blank.

Domino divination is best suited for seeking advice about specific situations, but it can also be used when inquiring about the current energies surrounding yourself. Dominoes are also the perfect choice for rounding out a séance where you have done another type of divination. They can provide you with warnings, advice, and words of encouragement.

There is a superstition that states that dominoes should not be consulted on Mondays or Fridays because they are inauspicious, but I could not find a source for this belief.

Many books on dominoes also discourage using your set for games, as it is seen as disrespectful. Frankly, I disagree. Joy and laughter are essential for the human spirit. Your tools gather your energy and are a reflection of your psyche; why not bring a little fun into the mix?

A brief history of domino divination

It is believed that dominoes originated in China. Written records about these small tiles date back to around the twelfth century, but it is likely they have been in use even longer than that.

Western dominoes, which are the type covered in this section, first appeared in Italy and then quickly made their way to France sometime in the 1700s. From there, the game made its way to England, likely brought by French prisoners.

The word "domino" may be derived from the domino cape, which is the black cape with white lining worn by priests. These special capes were also worn during masquerade balls in the eighteenth century, as well as by Venetian circus performers.

Different variations of dominoes have spread around the world since the nineteenth century. Many countries have their own specific games they play with the tiles.

One popular game in the United States and Latin America is called Mexican train. This game requires ninety-one dominoes and two or more players. It's believed that this game is derived from a Chinese game known as pai gow, introduced by Chinese laborers to Latin America in the mid- to late 1900s.

The fact that dominoes have captivated humans for so many years really speaks to their spiritual power. When humans were facing imprisonment and forced labor, they turned to dominoes for a sense of normalcy and comfort.

When you perform divination with a set of dominoes, you are connecting with the spirits and the legacies of many people.

How to perform a reading

1. Prepare and open your séance using the steps in chapter 5.

2. Place all your dominoes facedown on the table beside you. This group of tiles is affectionately known as the bone pile.

3. While focusing on your question or on the spirit with whom you want to communicate, mix the tiles around with your nondominant hand. If any flip over during this process, you can return them to the bone pile or accept them as part of your reading.

4. When you feel called to stop moving the dominoes, choose one to three tiles intuitively to answer your question or receive your message.

5. After you have interpreted the meanings, you can thank the spirits and close your séance.

TIP: Pull one domino a day and carry it around with you as you go about your routine. In the evening, take a few minutes to reflect on how its divinatory meaning applied to your day. This is a great exercise to try when you receive a new set.

DOMINO MEANINGS

The meanings of each domino vary greatly, depending on the literary source. The following dictionary contains the meanings that I personally use with my set.

0-0: This is the spirit tile. This can represent your spirit or the spirit of a deceased person or a guide. This tile serves as an acknowledgment that a spirit is present.

0-1: This tile warns that an enemy is in your midst. They are a threat to your security and happiness. Remain cautious.

0-2: You may be facing a period of financial difficulty. Be frugal for the next few weeks in case unexpected bills appear.

0-3: A hyperfixation on luxury and spending can bring other difficulties into your life, such as problems with relationships and friendships.

0-4: This is another tile that represents financial difficulties. Be sure you stay within your budget and be careful when signing any contracts.

0-5: Struggling with intimate relationships is a sign that you need to work on communicating. Make sure you spend as much time listening as you do speaking.

0-6: You may be the subject of rumors and gossip. Confront the one spreading misinformation head-on.

1-1: A happy reunion is going to take place. You may not have seen this person in quite a long time, so take care to really be in the moment with them.

1-2: This tile encourages you to spend time with your friends and loved ones. We all need human contact to thrive. Make your relationships a priority right now.

1-3: If you are considering switching careers or trying for a promotion, this is a very positive omen to receive. You may also be taking a trip related to your career that will open new doors.

1-4: Be cautious when it comes to purchases, and don't take on any new debts. This tile can also warn of taking on too much emotionally. Make sure that any bag you are carrying belongs to only you.

1-5: Love is in the air! A new romance is on the horizon, and it will be one full of joy and happiness. You may also be looking to rekindle a spark with an old love.

1-6: This tile is about all things relating to marriage and forming partnerships. If you have been hurt in the past, know that whatever relationship you are in now is a better fit.

2-2: Known as the wishing domino, the double twos are a wonderful domino to receive, especially if you have been going through a hard time. Don't give up: relief is on the way.

2-3: You have reached the end of financial hardship. If you have been waiting for a debt to be repaid, just know that it will happen soon.

2-4: Remain diligent when it comes to your money or personal belongings. Don't allow just anyone to have access to your home or personal safe.

2-5: This tile reminds us that competition is a part of life. Sometimes you win and sometimes you lose. If you have been passed over for an opportunity, just know that one that's better suited for you will come.

2-6: New opportunities surrounding your career are becoming available to you now. You may get the chance to collaborate with people you admire—don't let it pass you by.

3-3: Double threes are very lucky when it comes to domino divination. This tile represents windfalls and inheritances. Just remember that prosperity sometimes arrives in a form other than money.

3-4: You are very attractive and magnetic right now. If you are in a committed partnership, it should be going well. If you are single, someone may show interest in you soon.

3-5: If you receive this tile in your reading, you can expect a visitation from someone important to you. They could be living or dead. What is important is that you cherish the time together.

3-6: With numbers three and six, you can be sure to receive a gift. Whether it was expensive or not isn't important. What makes something truly valuable is the thought someone put into picking it out. Appreciate all you have for what it is.

4-4: A big party or celebration in your midst means it is time to let loose. This domino represents a gathering like a wedding, a new baby, or even a funeral. Celebrating life is important, even when it is attached to death.

4-5: If you have been hoping for a raise, now would be a good time to ask for it. Make sure you go into the discussion prepared. Be confident!

4-6: This tile asks you to reconnect with your inner child. What made you happiest in your youth? Find that joy once more.

5-5: A change of location is important now. This tile can also mean you need to look at a situation from a new perspective or frame of mind.

5-6: If you never make time to relax or unwind, it is only a matter of time before you become sick with stress. Make self-care a top priority now.

6-6: Everything should be smooth sailing now. Double sixes usher in positivity. If you have been facing uncertainty, just know that you will find the answers you seek when the time is right.

RECORD KEEPING

Date:

Time:

People present:

Tool:

Séance details (candles, heirlooms, etc.):

Spirits contacted:

Question asked:

Dominoes received:

Notes:

14

More Types of Scrying Divination

SCRYING DIVINATION

> **FIRE SAFETY:** Never leave a burning candle unattended.

This chapter will provide you with two forms of scrying: mirror scrying and candle scrying. I covered the definition of scrying in chapter 2 ("What Is Divination?" page 24), but essentially, it is the act of divining messages from a surface that is usually, but not always, reflective.

In both methods covered in this chapter, candles and candlelight play a significant role.

Candles have long been symbolic of a variety of things. They represent the human spirit, they represent divine knowledge, *and* they are thought to be a guide for ghosts who are traveling between worlds.

VANITAS, CANDLES, AND THE FRAGILITY OF LIFE

Vanitas are a works of art that fall into the broader category of still life. Still-life paintings focus on inanimate objects, usually ones found around the home. In vanitas, the objects are all connected to the delicate dance between life and death.

The ultimate purpose of vanitas is to show that life is fleeting and therefore should be appreciated. These paintings often showcase a series of specific objects, such as skulls, flowers, fruit, books, and candles. The candles (sometimes shown as lanterns) represent the soul of a person and are either depicted with a burning flame or with billowing smoke indicating that they have been recently extinguished.

Exercise: In your journal or records log, write down what you think the following items mean. This is good practice for when you need to interpret images while scrying.

Skulls, fruit, hourglasses, books, flowers, musical instruments, glassware, jewelry, and coins.

WHAT IS MIRROR SCRYING?

Humans have always been fascinated with their reflections. In Greek mythology, Narcissus is described as being so in love with his own image that he ends up drowning in it.

In many cultures, mirrors are thought to be beacons of truth, showing people what they may or may not want to see about themselves. Our reflections show us not only what we look like but also the depth and morality of our character.

Nowhere is this more true than in the story of Snow White, in which the evil queen asks her mirror the question "Mirror, mirror on the wall: who's the fairest of them all?," and she receives back an answer not to her liking.

But it isn't just looking at ourselves in pools of water and other reflective surfaces that has captivated us. No, it's the idea that secrets and messages can be revealed by them as well.

Mirror scrying, or catoptromancy, is the act of gazing into a mirror in order to see images or receive messages from the spirit world.

Mirror folklore

There is so much folklore surrounding mirrors that I could write an entire book on the subject!

Which beliefs do you recognize? Are their explanations similar to or different from what you were taught?

Breaking a mirror causes seven years of bad luck.

We can thank the Romans for this superstition. They believed that mirrors were used by the gods in order to observe human souls, so breaking one was disrespectful and would cause you to fall out of favor.

But where does the seven years come into play? Well, apparently the Romans believed that our lives and bodies renewed themselves every seven years. What is interesting is that the cells of the human body do actually replace themselves every seven to ten years.

Having no reflection means you have no soul.

This belief is a major part of vampire lore. Though variations of the vampire concept can be found across cultures, this specific superstition comes from the father of the modern vampire, Bram Stoker.

In his novel *Dracula*, the following scene is recounted by the book's protagonist, Jonathan Harker:

*This time there could be no error, for the man was close to
me, and I could see him over my shoulder. But there was no
reflection of him in the mirror! The whole room behind me was
displayed, but there was no sign of a man in it, except myself.*

Spirits can manipulate or get stuck in mirrors.

Covering mirrors in a home after someone has passed is a tradition found in multiple cultures.

In Britain and Ireland during the nineteenth and twentieth centuries, mirrors would be covered after a death as a precaution because it was thought that the spirit could get trapped inside them.

In those days, the bodies of the deceased would be displayed in the home, much as they are in funeral parlors today. It was assumed that during this visitation period, spirits were roaming the house, only to move on once their bodies were buried.

In Jewish tradition, it is common to cover mirrors after a death for the duration of the mourning period, which is known as shiva.

The reason for this is twofold. The first is that your appearance is not what is important and shouldn't be made a priority during this time. The second reason, which was more common in generations past, is a belief that mourning can attract malevolent spirits who can use mirrors to enter the world.

Bloody Mary…Bloody Mary…Bloody Mary…

The story of Bloody Mary, whose telling is a rite of passage for adolescent girls at slumber parties, is a staple in mirror divination folklore.

The rules of the game vary, but generally, it goes something like this: one person heads into a dark room alone, with only a candle to illuminate the space. Next, they stand facing a mirror and chant the phrase "Bloody Mary" either three or thirteen times (depending on the region where the game is played). After the final "Mary," a ghostly woman is supposed to appear in the glass. Depending on her mood, she then either provides you with answers to questions you have or claws your eyes out and leaves you for dead.

There are no definitively known origins to the Bloody Mary folktale, but it does have elements that recall catoptromancy. For one, performing mirror scrying was more common for girls than for boys. It was a rite of passage for a girl to conjure the face of her future husband in the mirror. And of course there was a macabre element to this practice, reminiscent of Bloody Mary, that said if a skull appeared to the girl, it meant she would die before she could wed.

Preparation for mirror scrying

Before we get to the steps, there is some important information to cover.

When mirror scrying, under no circumstances should you be intoxicated or under the influence in any way.

If you suffer from delusions or hallucinations, mirror scrying is not for you. I understand that this may be disappointing, but mental health must always be made a priority over practicing divination.

Mirror scrying, like automatic writing, takes a lot of practice and patience. It takes time for us to develop the skills required to really see, not just with our eyes but with our psyche. This type of divination requires you to trust your intuition, which can be a challenge for many people. If it doesn't happen for you right away, know that this is okay. Stick with mirror scrying for a minimum of one month before deciding it isn't for you.

Many people wonder what they will see during a scrying session, and that varies from person to person. You may see any combination of the following things: ghosts and spirits, objects, landscapes and other places, and shadow shapes.

If at any point what you are seeing feels negative, immediately end the session.

Objects and shapes are the most common things seen in mirror scrying, and they should be interpreted in a similar way as you would during a tea leaf reading. Feel free to use the dictionary from the tasseography section on pages 204–10 or the charm casting dictionary on pages 247–50 to help you interpret what you see.

Never do a mirror scrying session for longer than a few minutes. Because it is done in low light, you don't want to strain your eyes.

Choosing a mirror

Deciding which mirror to use is a very personal choice. Some people use whatever is on hand, while others have one they use only for divination.

If you would like to acquire a new mirror solely for scrying, you may want to try any of the following suggestions.

Heirloom: If you are lucky enough to have inherited a mirror from a friend or a close relative, this is the obvious choice when communicating with that person or others in the family.

Black mirror: Some people use special black glass mirrors for scrying. In Mesoamerica, circular black mirrors were made from polished obsidian and used for divination by the Aztecs and Mayans.

Circular mirror: Circles represent unity and wholeness. Because they have no beginning and no end, they are symbolic of life, death, and rebirth.

Rectangular mirror: Rectangles represent stability and security. Spiritually, they are the doors and passageways to the other side.

Square mirror: Squares represent equality and balance. They are a protective symbol, and each side can be a stand-in for one of the four elements: earth, air, fire, and water.

Triangular mirror: Triangles represent divinity and partnerships. Because they have three sides, they are symbolic of trinities, such as the Father, Son, and Holy Ghost in Christianity or the maiden, mother, and crone in witchcraft.

After you have decided on your mirror, you may want to energetically enhance it.

1. Charge or decorate your mirror with crystals. Placing a crystal on your mirror for a few days can boost its energy. Amethyst is a wonderful choice, as it is believed to enhance psychic activity. You can find crystal correspondences on pages 219–21 in the section about pendulums in the chapter on dowsing and pendulums (chapter 11, "Rhabdomancy").

2. Tie a colored ribbon to the mirror. Color is used frequently in witchcraft to enhance the energy of an object. You can choose based on personal preference or use the chart on page 76 (chapter 5, "How to Perform a Séance").

3. Sprinkle rose water or holy water on the mirror. This brings love, comfort, and security into your session. Roses promote tranquility, which is ideal for spirit communication.

Instructions

What's needed: a dark room, two candles, a mirror, a timer, and a piece of fabric to cover your mirror.

1. Gather your objects and open your séance by following the steps in chapter 5. You can set up everything with the lights on, including setting your timer for five minutes. After this is done, turn out the lights.

2. Place your mirror (covered by cloth) in the center of your work area and place a candle on either side. As you light your candles, you can focus on the spirit you would like to communicate with. If you have a specific question, now would be a good time to ask it out loud.

3. When you are relaxed and ready, uncover the mirror and gaze into it. Adjust the candle position if you need to. Your face should be illuminated, and there should be no need to strain your eyes. Take deep breaths and look at your face. Notice the way the shadows and light dance across your skin. Next, bring your attention to your eyes. Focus on them for a few breaths before letting your gaze relax.

4. Ask the spirit(s) to give you a message now. It may appear in the form of a distinct image or just a fuzzy shape in the shadows.

5. If your timer goes off before you have received an image, that is okay! Thank the spirit(s) and cover the mirror back up. You may wish to let the candles burn through or snuff them out, or you can continue on by trying candle wax scrying (see page 271).

6. You may now close your séance and work on interpreting the images you saw.

RECORD KEEPING

Date:

Time:

People present:

Type of mirror:

Séance details (candles, heirlooms, etc.):

Spirits contacted:

Question asked:

Notes:

CANDLE SCRYING

What is candle scrying?

In witchcraft, candles represent the element of fire. Fire is an integral part of life. It keeps us warm, it cooks our food, and it provides light in times of darkness. Without Homo erectus discovering how to harness fire for their benefit, who knows how Homo sapiens would have evolved? This history we have with fire obviously makes candle scrying a powerful form of divination!

Candle scrying can be done in a variety of ways, but the method I am teaching you is candle wax scrying, also known as carromancy.

Candle wax scrying is quite similar to tasseography, except instead of tea leaves in a cup, you are reading hot wax poured into a bowl of cold water.

I love candle wax scrying because it can be performed with items you already own or can purchase for less than five dollars.

A brief history of candle scrying

For the Ancient Greeks, Romans, and Celts, candle scrying was a popular form of divination. Each group had its own method, but the most well-known form is a type of candle flame divination called lychnomancy.

Lychnomancy likely began with the Greeks, but perhaps it evolved from a practice shown to them by the Egyptians.

Three candles are placed in the shape of a triangle on a table. As we learned from mirror scrying, the triangle represents the divinatory or the Holy Trinity. Next, a fourth candle is placed in the center of the triangle, and all are lit.

From there, the querent asks a question, and the movement of the center candle flame is to be interpreted for the answer.

Choosing a candle

Choosing the correct candle for your séance really comes down to personal preference and what is available to you.

Color

You may wish to incorporate color into your candle scrying, and you can either choose intuitively or use the color chart on page 76 to help you.

Scent

In witchcraft, the element of air is represented by scent. Air is much like the spirits: while you can't always see them, you know they are there. Air is both logical and psychic, just like divination.

Scent is a great way to connect to the spirits. If your grandmother loved to bake, an apple pie–scented candle can unlock powerful memories for you. Scents can also carry their own magical correspondences.

Lemon: Stimulating
Eucalyptus: Invigorating
Vanilla: Nostalgic
Rose: Loving
Rosemary: Protecting
Pine: Cleansing
Cinnamon: Warming
Lavender: Calming

Sigils

Sigils are magical symbols that can be drawn or carved into an object to enhance its energy. I have designed five for you that you can use for different types of readings.

 The spirit sigil: The spirit sigil can be carved into your candle when doing spirit communication readings.

 The love sigil: The love sigil can be carved into your candle when doing relationship or love readings.

 The health sigil: The health sigil can be carved into your candle when doing health-related readings.

The money sigil: The money sigil can be carved into your candle when doing career or finance readings.

The protection sigil: The protection sigil can be carved into your candle when doing any type of reading.

Inscriptions

Alternatively, you can inscribe your candle with names and words, such as a spirit's name, their birthday, or adjectives that describe them.

If doing a personal reading, you can carve the word "career," "love," etc.

A NOTE ABOUT WAX: Paraffin wax has been shown to be harmful to humans. When possible, opt for beeswax or soy-based candles with cotton wicks.

Choosing a bowl

The material that makes up your bowl represents the element of earth. In witchcraft, earth represents all that is material. It is a grounding and protective element, which is very important in spirit communication.

A water-safe container is all you need for a candle wax scry. It should be large enough that you have space for the wax but not so large that your image gets obscured. A standard cereal bowl is the perfect size for this activity.

If you wish, you can play around with the material of the bowl, trying different metals. You can find metal correspondences on pages 241–42 (in the charm casting section), but remember not to let water sit in metal for too long or you risk damaging the vessel.

Choosing water

The water in candle wax scrying obviously represents the element of water. This element is intuitive and emotional. Esoteric and spiritual knowledge is often depicted as being revealed by pools of water.

You can try incorporating different types of water into your reading:

Floral waters: The scent of flower-infused waters, such as rose water, can conjure specific emotions and memories.

Holy or blessed water: If you are religious, blessed waters are a great way to incorporate your own traditions into the séance.

Rain- or stormwater: Rainwater is representative of the heavens. It is a great one to try for spirit communication.

Lake water: Lakes have long been associated with other realms. They are thought to be home to different mythological beings.

Salt water: Salt water is not only spiritually cleansing; it also infuses your space with protection.

Instructions

Once you have picked a candle and all your accessories, you are ready to begin your séance.

1. Open your séance using the instructions in chapter 5 and prepare your workspace. You can turn the lights out or light a few candles to illuminate the room.

2. Quietly focus on the spirit you would like to communicate with, or if doing a personal reading for yourself, focus on the questions you have.

3. Next, place the bowl of water in front of you and light the candle you have chosen for the reading.

4. Slowly tilt the candle and allow the wax to drip into the water while you focus on your question.

5. When wax has filled about a third of the surface of the water, you may extinguish your candle and begin interpreting what you see. Use the tasseography dictionary on pages 204–10 to help you decipher the images!

Date:

Time:

People present:

Type of candle:

Type of bowl:

Type of water:

Séance details (candles, heirlooms, etc.):

Spirits contacted:

Question asked:

Notes:

STRENGTH

15

Caring For Your Tools

CARING FOR YOUR DIVINATORY TOOLS

Divinatory tools are the most important part of your séance, as they will be acting as the link between you and the spirits. This, of course, means that they are very hardworking and will therefore require special care.

It's important to understand that your divinatory tools all contain spirits of their own. Think of them not as inanimate objects but as companions who were created to work in conjunction with you.

Not only do they have spirits; they also contain the energy of their creator. Tarot and oracle cards are particularly prone to this phenomenon. The passion, dedication, and hopes for the deck are all embedded in its soul. When I created my deck the Memento Mori Oracle, I designed each of the cards with spirit communication in mind.

Because these tools are your companions, there needs to be a certain level of respect you show for them. Always make sure that you protect them not only physically but energetically as well.

GENERAL CARE: CLEANSING AND PHYSICAL PROTECTION

Your divinatory tools should always be safe in your care. This means it is your job to protect them when they are both in and out of use.

The first step you may want to take is dedicating an area for storage. Having everything in one place ensures that nothing is misplaced and also allows your tools' energies to mingle with one another.

> TIP: Always keep your tools out of sunlight, as this can fade artwork.

Always protect your tools from dust, dirt, and other debris. Make a point of cleaning their area often.

Take care while using your tools, but don't be afraid to actually use them. If I had a nickel for every time someone stopped using their tarot cards because they got a scratch, I would be a very rich woman. Think of every bend or scuff as a special memory or energetic imprint from a séance. However, there will come a point when a tool is too damaged to continue using. In this case, you should thank it for its service and retire it. Instead of disposing of it, try repurposing it in some way.

A chipped teacup once used for tasseography can become a small planter, and the pages of a book once used for bibliomancy can become wall art. Try to get creative with this task.

ENERGETIC CARE: CLEANSING AND SPIRITUAL PROTECTION

Because everything has a spirit, including your tools, protecting their energy is extremely important. Many emotions can arise during divination and spirit communication, and there may be times when you don't want them attached to your tools, or at the very least, you want the emotions to be settled and calm.

This is where energetic cleansing comes into play. There are a variety of

methods that get the job done, but the following three types are my personal suggestions.

Smoke cleansing: Passing a divinatory tool through incense smoke can remove built-up energy. The corresponding characteristics of different incense blends can be found on pages 76–77.

Crystal cleansing: Laying a clear quartz or selenite stone on your tools when they are not in use is an affordable (and pretty) way to both cleanse and protect them.

Sound cleansing: Ringing a bell over your tools is my favorite way to cleanse them. Sound is believed to change the frequency of an environment. Not only that, but bells have a long history of announcing death; what better way is there to cleanse your tools before a séance than by waking the dead?

INTERACTING WITH YOUR TOOLS

Something a lot of people overlook is the act of bonding with their tools. Of course, you are building a relationship with them in a session, but what about at other times? Here are my suggestions.

Take your tools on a field trip: One of my personal practices is to bring my tarot deck to the cemetery where some of my ancestors are buried. Try bringing your tools somewhere important to you; this could be a favorite park or a historical landmark.

Play a game with your tools: This is a controversial suggestion, but I think playing a game with your tools, such as a card game (as mentioned on page 82) or dominoes (page 252–53), is a great way to bond with them that also doubles as divination.

Treat them as friends: If you aren't sure what to do with your tools in order to bond, try treating them as people. What would you suggest you and a friend do on a Sunday afternoon for fun?

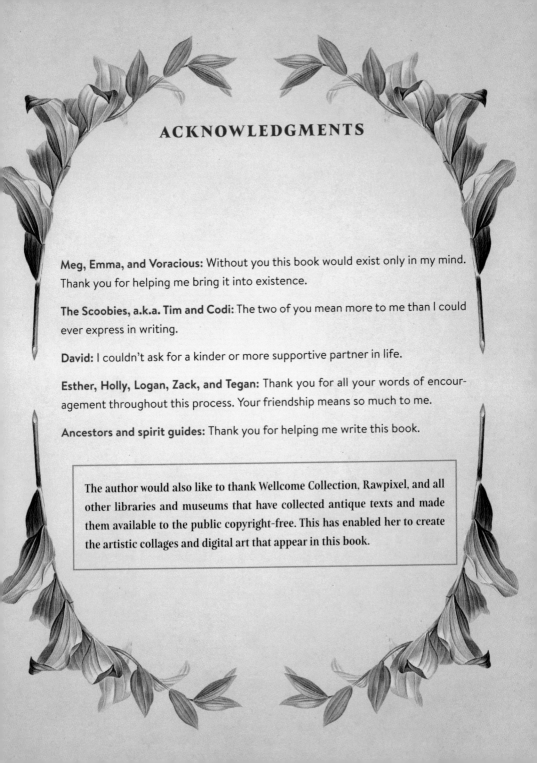

ACKNOWLEDGMENTS

Meg, Emma, and Voracious: Without you this book would exist only in my mind. Thank you for helping me bring it into existence.

The Scoobies, a.k.a. Tim and Codi: The two of you mean more to me than I could ever express in writing.

David: I couldn't ask for a kinder or more supportive partner in life.

Esther, Holly, Logan, Zack, and Tegan: Thank you for all your words of encouragement throughout this process. Your friendship means so much to me.

Ancestors and spirit guides: Thank you for helping me write this book.

The author would also like to thank Wellcome Collection, Rawpixel, and all other libraries and museums that have collected antique texts and made them available to the public copyright-free. This has enabled her to create the artistic collages and digital art that appear in this book.

GLOSSARY

Active: When a spirit manifests or communicates in some way with the living.

Afterlife: The realm or place the soul or spirit goes after the physical body has died.

Apparition: The ghost or ghostly figure of a deceased person.

Astral plane: The energetic level of the unconscious mind, ghosts, and spirits. Possibly where the afterlife exists.

Astrology: A type of divination that utilizes the movement of celestial bodies in order to make predictions about events.

Automatic writing: A type of divination in which messages from spirits are channeled through a living person onto a piece of paper in the form of writing or drawing.

Bibliomancy: A type of divination in which messages from spirits are presented to a living person through a passage in a book.

Cartomancy: A type of divination in which a person interprets a message through a set of playing cards.

Casting: Divination by choosing an item at random from a group of similar objects in order to make predictions.

Channeling: The act of receiving messages from the spirit world telepathically, psychically, or by way of a specific object or tool.

Clairaudience: The ability to hear information psychically.

Clairsentience: The ability to feel information psychically.

Clairvoyance: The ability to see information psychically.

Cryptid: A humanoid or animal figure whose existence has not been confirmed by science.

Demon: A supernatural being. In some religious denominations, a demon is a lower vibrational being who has the intent to hurt.

Divination: The art of interpreting signs and symbols in order to gain knowledge about the unknown or predict the future.

Doppelgänger: An exact copy of a still-living person.

Ectoplasm: A paranormal substance created by mediums while in a trance. Was popular during stage séances in the 1800s.

Elementals: A broad range of mythological beings such as fairies, imps, and other nature spirits.

Ghost: A physical apparition of a deceased person.

Intelligent haunting: The intentional interaction by a deceased person with a living person or environment on the physical plane.

Mediumship: The ability to communicate with the spirits or souls of deceased people.

Necromancy: The use of divination in order to communicate with spirits.

Nonhuman haunting: A haunting caused by a spirit that is not a deceased human.

Orb: A glowing ball of energy believed to be the spirit or soul of a deceased person.

Other side: The realm or place the soul or spirit goes after the physical body has died.

Paranormal: Phenomena that cannot be explained by current scientific methods or universal laws. Most often associated with ghosts and other supernatural beings.

Physical plane: The energetic level where the physical world exists.

Poltergeist: The physical manifestation of energy from a living person that causes changes in an environment.

Psychic: Having the ability to gather information through ways that are considered to be outside the natural laws.

Psychokinesis haunting: A poltergeist or other type of psychic haunting.

Rappings: Otherwordly knocks and tapping sounds that supposedly come from a spirit attempting to communicate.

Residual haunting: An energetic imprint on an environment that replays on a loop. It's generally acted out by an apparition.

Rhabdomancy: A type of divination in which messages from spirits are channeled through a set of rods or a pendulum.

Scrying: Divination by peering into a surface and seeing images that are then interpreted.

Séance: A session in which one or more people attempt to communicate with the dead by using spiritual or pseudoscientific methods.

Shadow people: A paranormal phenomenon of human-shaped shadow figures.

Spirit: The animating force that exists in all things, whether they are living, dead, or supernatural. Can be used interchangeably with "ghost" in some circumstances.

Spirit board: A board containing an alphabet and small phrases that is used to channel messages from a spirit. The most well-known spirit board is the Ouija board.

Spiritual plane: The energetic level at which universal law and divination are located.

Spiritualism: A religious movement in the nineteenth and twentieth centuries that focused on spirit communication.

Spiritualist: A person who believes that communication can take place between the living and the dead.

Stage séance: A type of séance at which a medium reads a group of strangers in an audience. Often contains elements of magic and illusion.

Table turning: A type of séance involving a group of people at which messages are channeled by a medium. Most popular in the nineteenth century.

Tasseography: A type of divination in which messages from spirits are interpreted by reading tea leaves or coffee grounds.

Veil: The boundary believed to be between the physical plane and the astral or spirit plane. The boundary that protects the living from the realm of the dead.

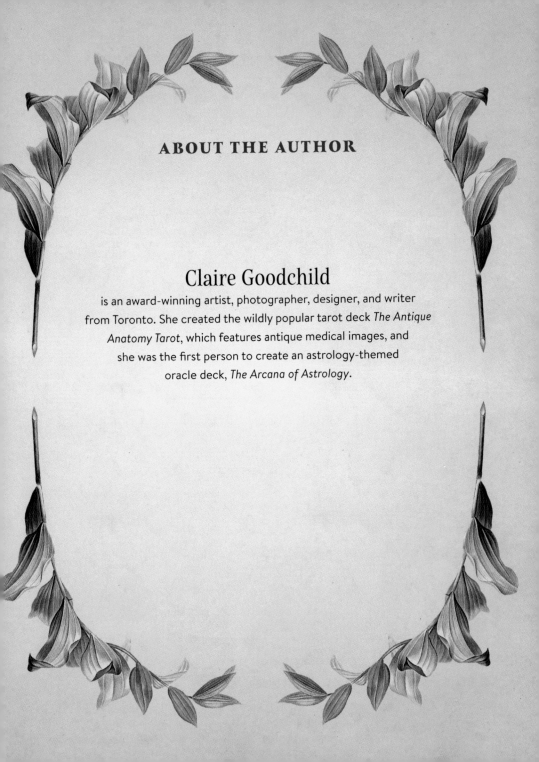

ABOUT THE AUTHOR

Claire Goodchild

is an award-winning artist, photographer, designer, and writer from Toronto. She created the wildly popular tarot deck *The Antique Anatomy Tarot*, which features antique medical images, and she was the first person to create an astrology-themed oracle deck, *The Arcana of Astrology*.

NOTES